The Feng Shui Factor

Modern Homes, Ancient Blueprint

MaryAnn Russell

1st WORLD
PUBLISHING

The Feng Shui Factor

MaryAnn Russell

© MaryAnn Russell 2007

Published by 1stWorld Publishing
1100 North 4th St. Fairfield, Iowa 52556
tel: 641-209-5000 • fax: 641-209-3001
web: www.1stworldpublishing.com

First Edition

LCCN: 2007930983
SoftCover ISBN: 978-1-4218-9965-7
HardCover ISBN: 978-1-4218-9981-7
eBook ISBN: 978-1-4218-9982-4

CONTENTS

*This book is dedicated
to the memory of Matt*

INTRODUCTION

Where we live, the homes we purchase, the importance of our living space and how we daily interact with our environment is the subject of this book. There is a "feng shui factor" to be considered when you analyze any home or property. People in the West are becoming more interested and knowledgeable about the practice of feng shui and applying its principles to their homes. There is a growing desire to grasp and understand this ancient Chinese art in order to make the best decisions about one's home and maximize the potential of one's living space. For most people, the purchase of a home will be one of their biggest investments and most valuable asset. It makes good sense to learn everything you possibly can about the "roof over your head." This book is an effort to mainstream the essential feng shui principles so that everyone can benefit from understanding this ancient art form.

For the Chinese, feng shui is part of a system of thought that seeks to understand the laws that govern the universe. The main challenge of teaching feng shui and more importantly *making it practical and useful,* in the West, is that it is part of a complex system of thought: an Eastern cosmology. The Chinese believe that there are **three main influences on our lives**, called the "**3 Lucks**". The **first** is the **heavenly influence** which is the divine-spiritual aspect of life. The **second** is the **human influence** which is character and personal development. The **third** is the **earth's influence** on life—the quality and level of harmony that we have in our environment. The Chinese believe we have control over the **later two influences**, human and earth, and it is from this that feng shui has its origins. By utilizing feng shui principles and analysis, a person is able to harness "**earth luck**" to enhance the quality of his or her life. The **human luck influence** incorporates some of the disciplines and practices we are more familiar with in the West such as: Chinese medicine, acupuncture, internal and external martial arts along with many other guidelines and teachings for developing one's potential. We will be exploring "**earth luck**" to assess what the feng shui factor of houses is all about. For our purposes, luck is best understood as a state of being ready when opportunities present themselves.

Feng shui is one of those subjects for which volumes can be written on a single concept. Additionally, feng shui, with all the various schools, systems and theories, can be contradictory and in the end result in more confusion than understanding. In this book, you will discover the "middle road" of feng shui. Why the middle road? If you stand in the middle of feng shui thought and chart a path to one edge, you may discover a very bleak prognostication of your home based on cycles of time and complex measurements with various interpretations. Setting out in the opposite direction and arriving at the opposite edge, you may end up in a fog of magical and superstitious thinking, wondering what really has merit and what doesn't. The good news is that nearly all feng shui teachings agree on what is called "**Form**" feng shui. Form feng shui deals with the relationship of the dwelling with its physical surroundings and includes house shape, flow, continuity as well as energy patterns and characteristics. In Form feng shui, contours of the land, waterways, hills, mountains, roadways and surrounding structures are all assessed to determine the safety and vitality of a dwelling.

We are going to explore the strengths and weaknesses of homes from the feng shui perspective, not from a design or architectural viewpoint. There will be commentary on design and architectural features but it will be solely from that of a feng shui consultant. My objective is to demystify feng shui and make it sensible and helpful for you in a contemporary setting. I want the reader to gain the greatest amount of understanding and practical application of feng shui as possible. I want you to be an expert when it comes to the essentials of feng shui.

The following material will provide you with a wealth of information about feng shui and how it applies to your living space. Studying this material will equip you to evaluate the most important features of any property. All of the essential feng shui principles and relevant topics will be systematically covered which will help you analyze the neighborhood, street scene and all of the exterior and interior features.

Throughout my years of feng shui practice and buying homes I can say with certainty that the insights and knowledge you gain from this book will greatly assist you in making a wise decision in what kind of home you choose to live. Once you have studied this material it is highly unlikely that you will find yourself saying, "Oh, I didn't realize this or that bothersome thing about the house or the neighborhood." Oftentimes, people will rationalize certain undesirable aspects of a house not realizing the impact it may have on their day-to-day life. Certain houses because of their configuration lend themselves more to struggle than to harmony. Also be aware that people can become accustomed to struggle and hardships, turning into a way of life for them.

A simple example would be the frustration of trying to back

your car out of the driveway every morning onto a busy street. Would you want to begin each day dealing with a potential hazard? There is a beautiful home on a canyon street in Los Angeles and it is apparent that feng shui has been expertly employed, but I always have the same thought when I drive by, "How frustrating it must be to pull out of that driveway." Having to cope with obstacles in your environment truly does have a wearying affect on your psyche. In the interior section on feng shui I will discuss the psychological aspects of feng shui, how on a daily basis décor, art and color have an influence on the unconscious mind.

We all desire our home to be a haven from the busy world, a safe and rejuvenating place where we can enjoy the company of our family and friends. Daily inspiration can be derived from being surrounded by the things that reflect and express who we are. Learning how to utilize the potential in your environment is one factor that can lead to greater purpose and satisfaction in all areas of your life. As it relates to your environment, this book will serve as a guide to a certain "quality of life." People who explore and study feng shui are looking to create a quality of life that is characterized by balance, success, health and fulfillment. Feng shui has its roots in a cosmology that presupposes that everything is interconnected and not separate, as we most often perceive it to be. Feng shui instructs us that because of the interconnectedness of all things our environments can have a profound impact on our daily life.

火 水 木 土 金

1. MAKING FENG SHUI PRACTICAL

Essential Concepts and Application

Throughout the book, essential **concepts** will be covered so that you will have a "context" for understanding this ancient Chinese art. The **concepts** will help you to understand the reasons why certain rules and guidelines are applied to the analysis of a home. While the concepts will be illuminating and informative they will also add to the depth and meaning of why and how we come to make adjustments in the environment the way that we do. In the text you will find the direct **application** of feng shui necessary to make adjustments that remedy the undesirable features and strengthen the areas that are weak. There are also separate **topics** that need specific clarification such as; stairways, mirrors, interior design etc.

The book is organized according to the method I have adopted when providing an onsite consultation. All of the information is compiled from my professional feng shui training, studies, research, colleagues, clients and personal experience. The information compiled here is what I consider *the feng shui essentials* that through your understanding can make a significant difference in the home which you are now living or one you may select in the future.

The Language of "Energy"

This book is written in the language of "energy." It will be the most used word in the book. Energy is a concept that suggests something that is intangible and can only be observed or experienced in its various forms and states. In everyday life energy is most apparent to us in its gross measurable forms such as geological phenomenon, weather systems, planetary movement and chemical, nuclear, biological, and electromagnetic to name a few. There are of course the subtler, less predictable and less calculable forms of energy in the subatomic world of quantum mechanics where only potentials can be theorized. We know that energy is neither created nor destroyed but it is endlessly transforming and being converted into one thing or another.

All of life can be characterized as an expression of energy. Whatever adjectives we use to describe life whether they are persons, places, things or experiences they all can be described with language that denotes some **energetic quality**. Life is an interplay and dance of energy from the observable and predictable to the hidden and inexplicable.

Feng shui teaches us to scrutinize the obvious visible qualities of an environment but to also evaluate the subtle, less obvious aspects of the living space. In feng shui we ask questions such as; how is the energy expressing itself in this home? Is it lively, calm, peaceful, chaotic, stagnate, harmonious, balanced or fluid? We understand that all things whether animate or inanimate have an energetic signature which influences the quality of the surroundings.

All the descriptions in the book whether they are cityscapes, landscapes, neighborhood settings, architecture, floor plan, the homes exterior or interior, room decor and design concept will ultimately be evaluated in terms of the quality, characteristics and the flow of energy. The individual aspects of the interior such as; art work, color and décor can be understood in the context of their energetic expression and influence. Feng shui at its core is entirely about the quality and expression of energy!

How to begin

The material that follows will equip you to make the best possible decision when selecting a home and it will instruct you on how to evaluate and practically apply feng shui to the home in which you presently live. If you are buying a home you won't necessarily be able to satisfy all the criteria that is discussed here, but you will greatly increase the odds of finding a home that has many of the essential feng shui features.

If you are looking for a home the surest way to proceed is to **know what you want in a home**. Make a sketch, find a picture or take a photo of a house that has the style you're looking for. Draw a floor plan and write a description of all the features you desire in a home. The fastest way for you to find a home is to be very clear about what you are looking for. Some people think the opposite is true, that if they desire too many features and are too specific they will never find "the house". In reality it doesn't work that way; most of the frustrations and delays that we experience in life come from *not knowing what we really want and not being clear and specific about it.*

Whether you are looking for a home or analyzing the one you have, use this book as a tool to sharpen your awareness about what you are seeing and feeling. Become aware of the features and design aspects of a house that are weak and lack fluidity or functionality. It is usually the *cumulative* effect of many weak feng shui features that will make living in the home difficult and consequently influencing the quality of your life. One of my master feng shui teachers would say to his students, "the first thing you must do as a practitioner is to stop the bleeding!" In essence, he was instructing his students to find the weaknesses and fix or minimize their influence. My desire for you is to gain the knowledge that is necessary to know what a house that has strong feng shui looks like and feels like.

It is quite possible that some of the descriptions that I give will describe where you are currently living. If you do discover that some of your home's features have weak feng shui do not let this disturb you. In most cases, there is a practical solution to make your home stronger. Also, as you read this book it is likely that it will help clear up any confusing feng shui ideas that you may have about your present home or one you may buy in the future.

火 水 木 土 金

2. Exterior Feng Shui

Macrocosm and Microcosm

In feng shui, we can analyze the environment in terms of the macrocosm and the microcosm. For the purposes of this book, you can think of your city and neighborhood as the macrocosm and your home as the microcosm. Of course, we can stretch out the macrocosm to be the state, country or hemisphere including the politics and culture but that is beyond the scope of this book. We are going to explore how the macrocosm, city and neighborhood, influence the microcosm, the home.

Neighborhoods

In order to make feng shui relevant and effective in the 21st Century, we have to consider all the things and technologies that didn't exist in ancient times. Industry, population, transportation and the way we use our utilities all have a huge impact on the energy of our homes and consequently on our health and well being. Here are the essential feng shui factors to consider when you are evaluating a neighborhood:

For a residence, the *continuity* of a neighborhood is important. Mixing commercial properties and or apartment/rental properties with single family home neighborhoods has two effects: the first is on the value and appreciation of the property for resale and second, on the daily experience of living with increased traffic, parking, noise factors, aesthetics, pride of ownership and general stability.

A neighborhood near the beach, or any recreational area, will have **seasonal changes** in the **population and density**. I recall a client who had a beautiful beachfront home and loved living there until the summer months, the time when she felt she had to escape from her neighborhood. For her, the serene atmosphere of her home was disturbed by a whole population of seasonal beach goers day and night.

Parking and access will always be a factor in high-density neighborhoods. One may want to ask if struggling to find a parking spot for yourself or your guests will be frustrating and limit the kind of lifestyle you desire.

A home located across from a school will be affected by parking, traffic and noise at different times of the day or evening. If the school has a large gym, a stadium or a theatre you could be faced with a constant flow of traffic near your home. From a feng shui perspective I tend to think it is too much of a disturbance for the harmony of the house.

Crisis Locations

Homes located near fire and police stations can be troubled by the continual interfacing with crisis, emergencies and criminality. Hearing sirens and emergency responders will put your body on alert and draw your focus toward crisis.

Additionally homes located near hospitals, cemeteries and mortuaries will be susceptible to the above conditions as well as an atmosphere permeated by sickness, death and grief. These things are part of life but we don't need to be living in close proximity to it. One thing we learn from feng shui is the balance of yin and yang* and hospitals and cemeteries are much too yin for the living.

Application

If you are living in a home that is located next to a hospital, mortuary or cemetery it is good practice to have an exterior light on 24 hours a day.

Pollution and Noise

Of course, there are the obvious pollutants such as power plants, dumpsites and land-fills that should be avoided. Additionally wherever there has been oil drilling, methane gases may be present.

Airport flight patterns bring noise and pollution. I had a client whose home was located near an airport and strangely it wasn't the aircraft noise that was the annoyance but the film of jet fuel that accumulated on the exterior of the house that concerned her. Other noise factors to consider are freeways, trains, stadium venues and amusement parks.

* See Appendix A

Utilities

Now that we've analyzed the characteristics that will have the greatest impact on the neighborhood, we start turning our attention to factors closer to the home. You can't change the neighborhood and some of the things that follow can be changed, but some things are as permanent as the neighborhood.

Inspect the neighborhood and area around your home for electrical grids, transformers, power stations, power lines and cell phone towers which can be disguised as redwood trees. The subject and debate whether or not electromagnetic fields* are harmful to our cells is ongoing. I would recommend living a distance of 2 miles from large transformers and electrical grids.

On the same subject of electromagnetic fields, if you are looking at a condominium or a townhouse, I suggest you check the location of the utility closet that services your building. The utility closet houses the power and electrical for the air conditioning, "tech center" and all the other utilities. The location of this closet is what gets tricky. Depending on the location it will usually affect the living space of one townhouse, more than another. These utility closets emit a high electromagnetic field and many of the newer developments that offer various amenities are designed in this way.

In one such case, it was fortunate that the high electromagnetic field (detected with a tri-field meter**) was confined to a walk-in closet and small sitting area. If it had been in the master bedroom, the client would have been sleeping in this high electromagnetic field. Unfortunately, the floor plan of the neighboring townhouse overlapped the utility closet in a way

* See Appendix B

** A tri-field meter combines magnetic, electric, and radio/microwave detectors in one device, so that the entire non-ionizing electromagnetic spectrum is covered.

that exposed a greater area of the living space to the electromagnetic fields.

As the public becomes more aware of the potential health risks about electromagnetic fields we may see a time when this could have an impact on the **value of the property**. In the future, sellers may find it difficult to sell a property located near transformers and other such utilities.

Power Poles, Trees and Vines

If a power pole, street light or any other immoveable structure is in line with the front entrance to the house it would be considered undesirable feng shui.

Large trees that are too close to the house may have to be removed in order to improve the feng shui. What is too close? When a tree or trees overpowers an area of the house by blocking the natural sunlight and energy, it will have an impact on the balance of the house by making it too yin. Also in feng shui, overly creeping vines are seen as parasitic and draining energy from the occupants of a home. In general, there should be a nice clear area in front of all windows and doors, free of any obstacles and impediments. This can be a sensitive subject for those who do not want to cut down trees or who like creeping vines. Certain areas require special permits to remove trees and it may even be unlawful to do so. The cost of tree trimming, maintenance and removal is something to consider when you are looking at the feng shui of a home.

The House Next Door

If the property lines in the neighborhood are close together it is best if the homes on either side of you are the same height or less. There will be an overpowering feeling if your home is dwarfed by the house next door. The case is worse if a single story home is between two 2-story homes. There are adjustments that can be made but it is rarely an optimum situation. A taller house to the rear of your home will be less intrusive from a feng shui perspective and will provide your home with the supportive "mountain form", which will strengthen the feng shui. In all cases living too close to a taller structure, hill or mountain will have a diminishing effect. This could express itself in your career and business affairs in terms of your confidence, authority and ability to influence situations and outcomes.

The Ebb and Flow of the Street

In urban and suburban feng shui, we examine the position of the home in relation to the streets, traffic patterns, surrounding structures and the overall configuration of the neighborhood. We look at the home in its setting to determine what influences are present. In a rural setting, the home is analyzed in relation to the mountains, hills, rivers and streams-just like in ancient times.

Houses located on the streets described in this section present the most difficult feng shui challenges. There are other subtle street patterns that can carry energy away from a house, but it does take a trained eye to detect them. In general, if you can avoid or correct the house locations described below it will be the most advantageous for you.

T - Intersection and houses on a curve

Houses located at the end of the dreaded "T" intersection should be avoided. The home will be continually assailed by the onslaught of traffic. The same can be said of a house located on a curve or at the end of a street. Cars driving around a curve, or in the direction of a home, will funnel a lot of force towards the house. This is unsafe, and causes a great deal of pressure for the occupants.

Application

The exterior of a home in this type of location can be improved by designing the hardscape or the landscape with curves so that the direct force of the energy from the street is deflected by the curved shape. Curved steps and half walls or a curved hedge will repel the onslaught of the street traffic and provide a protective barrier. I would recommend a 2-3 foot high hedge or half wall. You will have to study the direction of the traffic in order to strategically position whatever curved shapes you choose. The key is to meet the direct force with a curved shape.

Dead End Streets

Houses located at the end of a cul-de-sac or dead end street **do not have an optimum amount of energy flowing in the front of the home.** In modern feng shui, streets take the place of rivers and streams and are considered "virtual waterways". Streets move energy much like a natural body of water. When a house is located at the end of a street, with no outlet, the flow of energy is too slow, and tends to stagnate. This can be adjusted with feng shui but it is not a simple matter to fix.

Application

When a house is located at the end of a street, with no through traffic, something dramatic has to be done in order to enliven the energy. A tall tree, such as a Palm, or a flag pole that is strategically positioned will be the solution. The understanding is to lift up, the otherwise stagnate energy. Wherever there are towers, sky scrapers, flag poles and in a natural setting mountains and forests, the energy will be *naturally* elevated. A tall tree or edifice will naturally send the earth energy upwards and help to correct the stagnation that occurs at the end of a dead end street.

Below Street Level

Houses that are located below street level are very undesirable in feng shui. The energy of the home will not flow well and it could be hazardous. One could use the above remedy for elevating the "chi", but the house in general will be an unfavorable environment to live in.

Sloping Streets

If the street in front of the house slopes it may result in struggles with finances and career. As described above, the "virtual river" will move too quickly past the home. As you read further, **Feng Shui Concept #5** explains the necessity for energy to be **attracted** and **contained** in front of the home. **A sloping street in front** of the house doesn't allow the energy to pool, it just keeps moving like a river carrying potential opportunities with it!

Feng Shui Concept #1

Ideal feng shui form is described as having a mountain or hill in the back of the house for support, protection and stability. In ancient times, the back of the house was in the North, where there was a mountain or hill shielding the house from exposure to the cold northern winds. The front of the house would face the South where the warm gentle breeze would disperse the vital energy that gives life to all. On either side of the house, there would be a hill to the East and a smaller hill on the West side. In effect, the house would be situated in this "arm chair" shaped landscape, protected and supported on all sides. There would be an expanse in the front with a gently flowing stream or river that would attract abundance to the home. The front entrance is open and receptive to the warm gentle wind (feng - wind) which interacts with the stream or river (shui - water) dispersing the vital chi. This Chinese poem says it best,

"The winds are wild...The sun is warm...The water is clear...The trees are lush"

This illustration depicts all the elements that are optimum for strong exterior feng shui.

In a suburban or urban setting the movement created by the street in front a house acts like a virtual waterway; the neighborhood setting, surrounding structures and landscaping are substituted for the natural land forms.

Homes that back to a street (virtual waterway) do not have the support or stability of the mountain (still and solid) in the rear.

Additionally, a property where the **rear sharply drops off** to a cliff does not meet the mountain criteria. For our modern times, a home that is located on an interior street of a neighborhood will be best. Also, when the landscape in the rear of the home has an upward slope or terrace the feng shui form will be enhanced.

In feng shui, **corner lots** are seen in general as having **too much exposure**. Also, homes have a male (yang) and female (yin) side. As you are standing with your back to the front door, facing the street, the right side is the feminine side and the left is the masculine side of the house. Having a home adjacent to a busy street will disturb the balance of yin and yang. One side will be more active than the other resulting in some type of need to compensate for this imbalance. Of course, there are the obvious noise factors to contend with whenever a home backs or sides to a busy street. With careful attention to the design of the landscape and the hardscape, the *over exposure of corner lots* can be minimized. The solution would be to utilize the landscape to absorb, buffer and shield the home from too much exposure.

Feng Shui Concept #2

Essentially feng shui is about balanced energy. Where there is too much energy it can be slowed down, reduced, softened or redirected. If energy is too slow or feels stagnate, it needs to be enlivened. When the energy is chaotic and going in different directions, it can be guided and directed. All this managing of energy movement can be accomplished with careful attention to architecture, landscape, design, furnishings, art, color and texture.

Rural to Urban

Most of my feng shui consultations are in urban and suburban areas but often enough my consultations take me out to a ranch or a mountain cabin. The following are some basic things to be aware of in a rural setting that you wouldn't find in a suburban setting:

1. Rivers and lakes in close proximity to the house that have the potential to over flow. Additionally, a river in the rear of a house can weaken the feng shui but there are exceptions to this.

2. A mountain top house that is overly exposed.

3. Barns that are poorly situated in relationship to the house.

4. Septic tanks that are poorly situated in relationship to the house.

5. Ample forest clearing around the house to avoid fire hazards or trees that overshadow the house.

6. Overshadowing hills, boulders or other land formations in close proximity to the house.

The key is to study the land formations in a rural setting to make sure the house is not over powered by the landscape.

Waterfront Homes

The ocean is obviously a powerful source of energy and I think the biggest challenge living in a beach front home is fine tuning just how much of that energy the house is exposed to. Too many "floor to ceiling windows" facing the ocean will over stimulate the house thereby sacrificing a comfortable and cozy atmosphere. If the energy is not well contained through design and décor the occupants may experience a lack of stability in the rise and fall of the tides.

The best location for a house in a harbor or marina is in a channel that isn't too busy. Boat fumes can be noxious in a busy harbor and the accumulation of fuel and other pollutants is always more apparent on channels where there is no outlet. Examine the harbor the same way you would a street in a neighborhood.

In general, "water" is connected with our emotions and some people can be more sensitive to water's influence than others. In Chinese medicine, the element of water relates to the kidneys and the corresponding emotion of fear.

Application

Placing potted plants and trees on balconies and decks will help absorb the **influence of too much water**. Strategically placed objects made of stone will also help stabilize exterior areas of the house that may be overly exposed to the elements.

High Rises

A high rise lacks a connection with the earth, so it is important to pay special attention to incorporate nature's earth elements into the décor. The view in a high rise will have the greatest influence on the energy of the space. A 180 degree view can create an excess of energy and it will be difficult for people to relax, concentrate and focus. Remember to avoid a location near an elevator. Make sure that your front door is not opposite another door or entrance and that the hallway to your front door does not feel claustrophobic or stagnate. High rises can have high electromagnetic readings because of shared utilities. Use a tri-field meter and check the shared walls and in particular, the wall where you are sleeping. Parking and easy accessibility in a high rise should be considered in terms of your lifestyle, such as your daily routine, family life and entertaining.

火 水 木 土 金

3. What's in Shape?

Lot Shapes

Lot shapes and where the house is situated on the lot is very important. This is one of the feng shui factors that requires close attention. There is very little one can do to correct the shape of a lot or how the home is situated on it. In nearly all cases where an irregular lot shape is in question, the balance of the house will be off. The following examples and descriptions will help you analyze the home's position on the lot and detect whether the lot has an irregular shape.

In **example #1**, the house is obviously poorly situated on the lot. It is clearly out of balance with the *whole* and will affect the masculine and feminine dynamics in the home. The lot itself is shallow and without depth which would make it difficult to contain the energy.

In **example #2,** the lot shape is very good but the home is situated too close to the front of the lot. The front of a house should always have sufficient space for energy to gather and accumulate. If the space in the front of the house is inadequate, then opportunities will be whisked away too quickly. Additionally, when the house is situated so that the front yard is spacious, the depth will create a natural protection for the front of the home and in particular the front door.

#2

Feng Shui Concept #4

The aim of feng shui when you are analyzing the **front of a house** is to:

1. *Attract* "chi" energy

2. *Contain* or pool the energy in the space in front of the house

3. *Draw* it in the front door

This can be achieved with balanced landscaping and a well designed walkway to the front door. The energy will be ***attracted*** to the house and ***contained*** through the landscaping, and then the energy can be ***directed*** to the front door via the walkway. Conversely, if the front yard is shallow and not enhanced with the appropriate landscaping the energy will be ***attracted*** but it won't have a ***container (yard and landscaping) to hold it and then direct*** it to the front door.

In **example #3,** a section is missing in the lot and in **example #4,** it is misshapen and narrow in the rear. Try to avoid these kinds of misshapen lots, if they have large sections missing, or they dramatically narrow off on one side they are extremely difficult to correct with landscaping. The goal is to find a property that is optimum, and I have never felt confident these misshapen lots have good feng shui. They tend to imbalance the entire house.

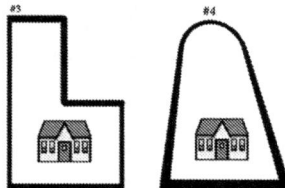

In **example #5,** the home is nicely situated on an evenly shaped lot. There is sufficient space in front of the home for energy to gather and pool. Adequate frontage provides space for a well-designed landscape that will help buffer the front of the house from the external elements. The equal space on the sides of the house will add to the interior's balance, particularly in terms of the balance between masculine and feminine. The depth in the rear creates strength, stability and support.

#5

House Shapes - A Seamless Whole

Irregular Floor Plans

Irregular floor plans and missing sections of a house can weaken the feng shui.

The most important thing to evaluate is how truly irregular the shape of the house is. The key is to have a seamless whole so that the energy flow is even and unimpeded. If the design is lopsided, asymmetrical and unbalanced there will be parts of the home that feel harmonious while other sections will lack energy and flow. Some house shapes can be so disjointed that certain areas don't feel part of the house.

Missing Areas

Missing sections have always been a concern for those trying to achieve optimum feng shui. While most homes have missing sections, the key is to weigh how much of the missing area is affecting the 'whole'. If the missing section is *dramatic*, it can sometimes be correlated to a weakness in a life aspiration*, an individual family member or a part of the body.

The following examples 1-7 will give you an overview of how irregular shaped houses influence the flow and quality of energy in the living space. When studying these shapes think of the gray areas as making up the 'whole' and contrast it with the irregular shapes and missing sections. In feng shui, shapes and forms are interpreted and given meaning. Some of the house shapes have been given labels such as; a cleaver, a boot or an "L". The idea is that no one wants to find himself on the wrong end of the cleaver's blade or the boot's toe or heel. Let's look at each of the examples below.

Example #1

The missing areas of this house are not too dramatic in this example. The multiple angled walls are the big challenge for this house shape. The slanted gray lines depict the skewed energy flow that is a result of angled walls. The area that extends beyond the whole or otherwise even shape is simply an *extension*. An area is considered an *extension* when its width is 1/4 to 1/3 of the whole. In most cases extensions can be considered an expansion of that particular area and be beneficial.

* See Appendix C

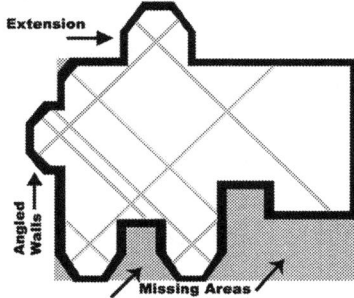

Example #1
Angled Walls

Extension

Angled Walls

Missing Areas

Example #2

The "L" shaped house in this example leaves the back without support. There is no true "commanding" point in the rear of this house shape. In this case the "L" shape leaves a vacuum in the rear where there should be structure and stability.

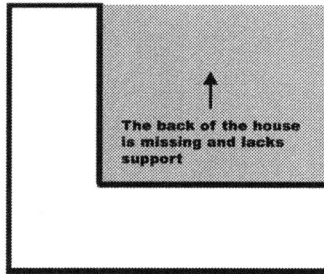

Example #2
L- Shaped House

The back of the house is missing and lacks support

Example #3

The "L" shaped house in this example reduces the flow of energy to the front of the house. In cases like this the front door is hindered by the protruding structure. Secondly, houses with this configuration have challenges separating the driveway and cars with the path to the front entrance. The overlapping area can leave cars pointed at the front of the house, which is never a good idea.

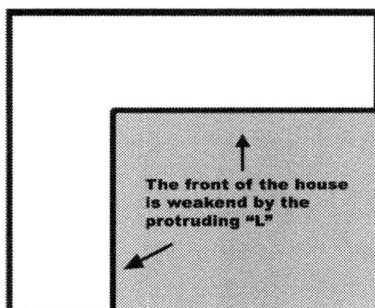

Example # 3
L-Shaped House

The front of the house is weakend by the protruding "L"

Example #4

The boot shape in this example has a significant missing area at the top while the bottom "toe" section has an extension. Remember that extensions can be considered an expansion of a particular life aspiration, such as; an extension in the north can give the career area greater emphasis. In this example, the line from the 'heel' to the 'toe' is mostly even with the extension under the toe area. The heel or toe section is considered the weakest area of the boot shape, particularly for a front entrance or a bedroom location.

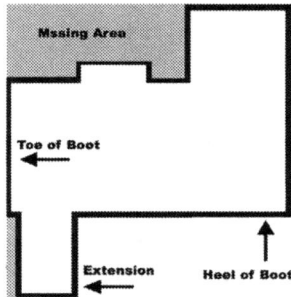

Example #4
Boot Shape

Mssing Area

Toe of Boot

Extension   Heel of Boot

Example #5

Contrast the irregular shape and missing areas to the completeness of the gray outline. The bottom of the house shape looks like it a "bite" has been taken out of it. A house with these irregular lines will be very challenging to correct with feng shui. The best solution is to have the walls pushed out to create an even line. Focusing a remodel to correct the irregular shape of a house and gain optimum feng shui form is an excellent way to maximize your remodeling dollars.

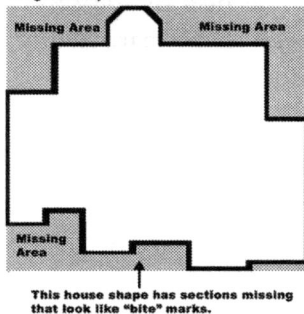

Example #5
Irregular Shape

Missing Area   Missing Area

Missing
Area

This house shape has sections missing
that look like "bite" marks.

Examples #6 & 7

The cleaver shaped houses have many missing sections as well as a lack of symmetry and balance. In terms of the missing areas, example #7 is less severe in its shape and appears more complete, although I can still detect the shape of a cleaver. Example #6 is seriously lopsided on nearly every side. It is very difficult to correct shapes like this with feng shui placement alone, some remodeling will be necessary in order to unify the disparate parts and bring 'wholeness' to the structure.

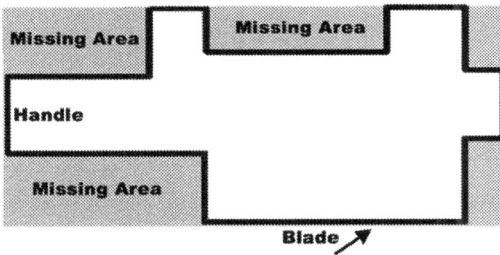

Example #6
Cleaver Shape

Missing Area

Missing Area

Handle

Missing Area

Blade ↗

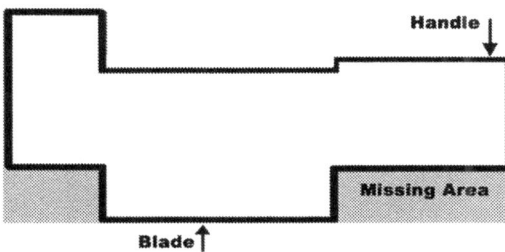

Example #7
Cleaver Shape

Handle ↓

Missing Area

Blade ↑

I hope this section has added to your ability to detect irregular shaped houses. With your focus on balance, symmetry and 'whole' shapes it will be easier to see whether a house has a lopsided shape and appears to be missing large areas. It's important to note that the natural movement of energy will tend towards the areas of the house that are the most symmetrical and balanced. While the sections that are dissimilar and feel disjointed from the rest of the house will lack flow and continuity. It's challenging to keep energy balanced and flowing in these sections of the house because they are somewhat disconnected from the 'whole'. People will often find it difficult to come up with just the right design concept for these areas. When I hear the comment, "this room just never seems to come together", I realize this can be a symptom of stagnate energy. I then focus on the shape of the room or area and analyze how it's connected or not connected to the rest of the house.

Application

What to do with the irregular shapes? There are two ways of looking at correcting irregular shapes. One is to even out the line of the house using landscaping tricks and secondly filling in the space as if it is part of the house. In other words you are seeking a way to shape and form what is missing and then to unite it with the 'whole'. With landscaping you can create a permanent border using a hedge, trees or half wall with brick or stone. Something less permanent can be used such as landscape boulders, stone pillars, large ceramic pots and pedestals. Once the missing area is complete with a border the space should be filled in. A seating area can be created with a colorful outdoor rug. A rock garden with a bench, an oversized umbrella, canopy or lattice work will fill in the space. Whichever design concept you choose, focus the placement towards the house. Angle the furniture and landscape objects inward. This will subtly direct energy toward the house and help unify the missing area. See the example below.

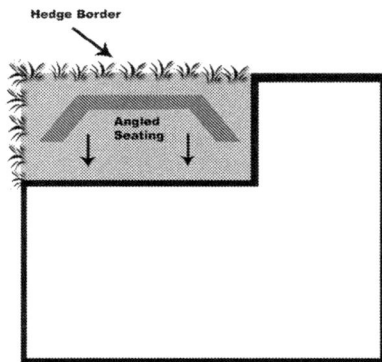

Hedge Border

Angled Seating

Room Additions & Remodeling

I want to offer a cautionary note about adding structures to a house. Adding on to a house without considering the impact on the shape and layout of the house may weaken the feng shui. Sometimes people plan additions with a narrow focus in mind, without looking at the *whole*. In most cases the size and shape of the lot will dictate where the addition can be added.

Here are some examples of what I consider to be feng shui missteps in the area of remodeling and additions:

1. Adding square footage to a home throughout the years and ending up with a floor plan that is fragmented and disjointed. This undercuts the value of the home, makes it difficult to sell and seriously challenges the feng shui.

2. Adding onto the second story that makes a home ill-shaped and top heavy. From a feng shui perspective this would be akin to being overloaded without an adequate foundation for support.

3. Converting the master bedroom into a master "suite" by extending it over the garage. Having the sleeping area over the garage creates instability.

4. Replacing the front door with French doors. Feng shui considers "the front door" one of the key features of the home. Thus adding more access points to the front of the home will confuse the energy.

5. Adding a detached structure (guest or servant quarters, office, workshop, studio or retreat) **without connecting it to the main house via a walkway or specified path.** Detached structures on the property may challenge family cohesion or in the case of employees, act too independently or countermine the employer.

6. In an effort to create an "open" floor plan key areas can be overly exposed by knocking down walls and adding too many doors or windows. One such example: opening the kitchen up to the point of being able to see it from the front door. As you read further you will understand how this affects the feng shui. It becomes very difficult to contain and manage the energy in a home where there are too many windows and doors.

7. Adding on to the front of the house so that it obstructs the visibility of the front door. I knew a contractor who basically ruined the feng shui of his house by adding on to the front of his home. It is unfortunate because the view of the front door is now hidden from two different angles due to the obstructing add-on. The best solution in this case will be to move the front door and create a new entrance.

8. Remodeling a home to the point where it is over-built for the neighborhood is more of a real estate and financial issue than a feng shui one. Although, I have seen neighborhood relations turn hostile as a consequence of over-building. This type of animosity will most certainly affect the balance and quality of life. It is advisable to know what the CCR's (Covenants, Conditions and Restrictions) allow for building modifications before you purchase and also if the extent of your remodeling will be a good financial decision in terms of real estate value.

9. When a home is extensively remodeled and significant square footage is added, the front door is dwarfed and ill proportioned to the rest of the house.

The basic **bones** of the house should be the guidelines and parameters for the addition or remodel. Unless you are completely rebuilding the house, the integrity of the original design should be improved or left intact. One should never be able to detect where additions have been built. I have observed extensive remodels that have far exceeded the original design and the feng shui of the home was left compromised. If after studying this material you still have questions about your remodeling project, it would be best to get professional advice while you are still in the planning stages. I believe you obtain the most from your remodeling budget by focusing on the changes that will enhance the feng shui of your home.

火水木土金

4. Easy Access — Easy Life

Accessibility and the "Front Door"

Now that we've covered the neighborhood setting and detailed the things that have the greatest impact around the property, we've arrived at the **Front Door**. In simple terms, it should be very easy to find and access your front door. When approaching a house it must be apparent where the path is to the front door. Being able to see the entrance is optimum but secondly a person approaching your home should not be confused or have to guess which direction will lead them to the front door.

Your front door, in all cases, should make a strong statement and be distinct in some way. The aim is to attract positive Chi (energy) to the front door. Choosing a home where the front door is hidden by the garage or by a low hanging roof line is very weak feng shui. Homes that have a *front door* but also have French doors opening up to a front patio will confuse the energy of the home. In feng shui a home must have only one front door.

Town homes, Condominiums and Apartments

Choosing a town house, condominium or apartment that has good access is a very important feng shui factor. In these situations, having a visible and easily accessible front door is usually the greatest challenge. Does the front entrance of the apartment or condo satisfy **feng shui concept #5**; the attracting, containing and drawing in of energy? There is also the *feng shui psychology* to consider; having an arduous climb to get to the front door may entrain a pattern of struggle in your life. If, when walking out the front door, the first thing you face is a wall or a fence your psyche will register blockage, obstruction and blankness. The same will be true of a first floor entrance where the front door opens to the stairway of the unit above it. In all of these cases, feng shui adjustments should be made to ensure easy access and remove any sense of obstruction. Also note that homeowners associations in these communities are usually strict and you will have to be very creative in order to make your front door distinct.

Pathways and Entrances

Pathways to the front door that are impeded by over grown foliage, vines and trees should be trimmed. One should never have to duck under or walk around a hanging plant or vine when approaching the front door. Stand on the sidewalk and check the entrance from all angles to make sure the entrance and the path to it is visible and unobstructed. After sunset, the path to the front door should be well lighted. A driveway should never overlap onto the walkway allowing a car to be parked facing your front door.

Application

An **exterior stairway** to the front door needs to be energized by **bright colors and movement** to help guide the energy up the stairs. Psychologically this will make the ascent up the stairs easier as well. The object that you choose will depend on the space. Some suggestions are: brightly colored ceramic pots, landscape statue, chime, windsock, flag, large outdoor rug or mat, flowers and greenery.

If you face a wall, fence or other obstruction when you walk out the front door the key is to **place something that immediately captures your attention**. A potted tree, a colorful textile or any one of the suggestions above will avert the eye, and thereby the message of "blankness or blockage."

The Front Door

The material and design of the front door is important. To maximize the feng shui of a house, the front door must give the sense of strength, protection and power. A beautifully designed solid wood front door is the best choice. Choose high quality hardware that enhances the door, further giving it an appearance of strength. Metal front doors that are designed to look like wood are also very strong and durable and may be more suitable for some climates.

The **red front door** symbolizes protection and power while energizing the luck of the house. It is certainly eye catching, but it is not necessarily within the aesthetic sensibility of everyone or always compatible with the compass direction it is facing.

Application

A red front door is very useful when the front door is partially hidden because of the design of the house, or if there is some other external obstacle impeding the energy flow to the front door.

Glass front doors do not fall within feng shui design. They will leak energy. Front doors made of beautiful etched glass do not have the strength that a solid wood door has. In the interior section of the book, I will discuss how glass can sometimes be viewed as "breakable chi or energy." Slanted or angled front doors can be problematic throwing off the overall alignment and balance of the house.

Application

Good feng shui can begin or end at the **front door**. The goal is to have a strong, accessible, inviting and safe front door entrance. The front door should always be in good repair. Make sure the porch lighting is adequate (replace burnt out bulbs). The door must never stick or be a struggle to open and all the locks should work properly.

Another way to examine a property from the front door is to stand with your back to the front door and look at the view. Professional feng shui consultants will do this and in some cases take their compass reading from this location. Inspect the roof lines of the houses across the street to make sure that points or "poison arrows" as it is called in feng shui are not attacking your front door. Check to see if it is pleasant and peaceful with a feeling of safety. This is a kinesthetic or visceral exercise to observe the feelings in your body to get a sense of a house. Some people are more practiced at this than others. Children tend to have less filtering and mental activity going on than adults do, so it is helpful to observe their response and consider their feedback.

火 水 木 土 金

5. A Homes History

The Predecessor - Who has lived here before?

The "predecessor" energy as it is called in feng shui will give you some understanding about the property, as the overall condition of the property will tell you something about the prior owner. It is good investigative work to learn what you can about why the house is being sold. If it is a new construction it is worthwhile to find out about the builder and how successful his developments have been. With a newly constructed house it is not as important but some information is helpful. Are you the first to make an offer? Which phases or plans have been most in demand, etc.?

In the state of California, the owner has to disclose whether anyone has died in the house. I also know that the insurance commission keeps records of homes that have had *repeated* claims for water damage due to plumbing and faulty pipes. If the flooding has been extensive, the foundation of the house may be compromised or there may be issues of mold. Issues of water damage, fire and death all fall under the *homes history* and it is something to take note of. Your professional home inspector will advise you on the condition of the house, needed repairs and anything that does not meet the building code.

Application

Think of this as information gathering and research. Don't get caught up in trying to draw conclusions about the property based on the predecessor or any other single aspect of a house. Remember you will be basing your decision on the "whole" picture. This information is intended to equip you to see the big picture when you are looking at a property.

Generally speaking, I have been able to correlate the predecessor factor to business locations more than to homes. Some business locations have one failed business after another and this can be easier to track because of the short time span. The reasons some business locations have weak feng shui are more obvious. Things like visibility, accessibility, parking and the surrounding buildings are all general factors to consider regardless of the type of business. The story you always want to hear from a business location is that the previous business quickly out grew the space! The same is true for a house; when the reason the house is being sold is because the owners are moving to a larger home you can consider this a plus.

Case 1

A long time family friend has lived next door to a house whose occupants have had two divorces within 10 years. After the two divorces, the house was sold and completely remodeled during which time no one occupied the house. The newly remodeled house was sold again, completely demolished and rebuilt but still remains unoccupied. After observing 17 years of bizarre history with this house one may conclude that this is not a desirable house to live in.

Case 2

In a recent consultation with a client we were able to determine that she and her husband were the third owners of a 12 year old home. This sprawling custom built home had some very weak feng shui design features, particularly in the master suite. I recall that the two previous owners had sold the house due to divorce. Fortunately for my client, she had enough knowledge about feng shui to convince her to work with a professional in the hope that her life in this home would have a much better outcome than the previous two owners.

Application

To be cautious, if a house has been sold more than two times within 10 years for reasons of divorce or chronic illness I would consider this inauspicious. Always find out **how long the owner has lived there and their reason for moving.**

The home's history is something to consider but not always relevant. Individuals and the homes they are drawn to are a host of "potentials" yet to unfold. Sometimes it can be very obvious why a home has an inauspicious history, as in **case 2**, while other times it remains a mystery, as in **case 1**.

6. – Interior Feng Shui

The **interior** section of this book will cover the feng shui factors that have the greatest influence on your environment. You will find suggestions and tips on how to make adjustments to your living space. Generally speaking, it is easier to make feng shui adjustments to the interior of a home than the exterior. Minor exterior adjustments involve landscape modifications, placement of water features, refurbishing and general up keep and repairs. Major exterior changes usually involve construction and remodeling. A potential house may have feng shui challenges with décor, furniture placement or otherwise minor fixes and may be a very good house. The material that follows will help you to see and understand the more subtle aspects of your home.

Feng Shui and Interior Design

I must begin by saying that a feng shui practitioner is not an interior designer and an interior designer is not a feng shui expert. Both of these fields can overlap and complement each other but they should each be studied exclusively in order to truly gain expertise in both.

A feng shui expert will firstly relate essential feng shui principles to a home's design and layout. After analyzing a property using fundamental feng shui precepts, a practitioner will make recommendations to adjust, correct and enhance the feng shui. Recommendations can come in the form of repairs, remodeling, painting, adding or changing color, landscape design, placing objects of art, rearranging furniture, removing furniture and objects of art and placing water features or other various elements. In general, *the feng shui expert is trained to assess how energy is expressing itself in the environment and determine what the influence is on the occupants.* The practitioner will then use a variety of the above elements with the objective of finessing the energy in one way or another to satisfy some feng shui criteria. Aesthetics and design elements are used by the feng shui expert to achieve good feng shui but the practitioner doesn't approach the space with design as the primary focus. Design concepts and décor are tools for the feng shui practitioner to utilize.

An interior designer is trained to focus on design, décor and aesthetics. In many cases, it is best to use the expertise of a professional interior designer to create a design concept or come up with an idea that **solves a feng shui problem**.

It is important to distinguish between these two fields; the feng shui expert usually does not have the extensive design background or experience and the interior designer, while only focused on the design concept, may be untrained in the subtle aspects of feng shui and weaken the house.

Feng Shui Concept #6

When the **interior energy flows well** in a home it is best characterized as a "meandering" stream. People will be able to move about the house freely. A natural calm will be present and the environment in general will feel open and spacious. Conversely, some houses have an ambient sense of pressure, compression and tension. This is a result of an imbalance in the flow of energy throughout the house. Where there is an *excess of energy* it is difficult for people to relax and focus. If the *energy is stagnating*, the environment will lack vitality, creating a mood of inertia. Striking a balance, where the energy is neither excessive or stagnate is the goal of feng shui. (see **feng shui concept #2**).

Entrance Hall

The foyer or entrance hall of a house should be open, inviting and well lighted. The first thing I look for on a consultation is whether I am able to "pause" in the entryway of a house. This is a *subtle* but very good indicator whether the house is balanced. Some entrance halls feel as if you must quickly make your way to another room once you've entered the house. This rushed unsettled feeling can be due to a number of things: the entrance may be cramped or cluttered by furniture, the stairway may be facing the front door, the back door may be directly in line with the front door and the hallway between them is direct, narrow or funneled. There may be statues or mirrors that are over powering when you first walk in. Certain objects of art may be unsuitable for the entrance and better placed in another part of the house.

Let's discuss the top 5 challenges to entryways in feng shui:

1. The stairs face the front door
2. The front door and the back door are directly aligned
3. There is a bathroom too close to the front door
4. There is a bedroom too close to the front door
5. The kitchen is too close to the front door

In feng shui a stairway can be compared to a virtual waterfall. As in nature, moving, rushing water, whether it is a wave, river or waterfall can be powerful and uncontrollable. The most you can hope to do is deflect or divert its course in another direction.

When a **stairway faces the front door**, the waterfall effect pushes the *energy* back out of the front door. If you will recall, in **feng shui concept #4,** when we speak of *energy*, we are talking about all the things that contribute to an abundant life: health, wealth and relationships. This happens in two ways: the front door will leak wealth and opportunities that have been gathered or when opportunities and good fortune are attracted to the front door, they will be pushed out by the rush of opposing stairway energy. Either way, they both add up to struggle when it comes to holding onto money and opportunities.

Stairways

Stairways are best located somewhere off the center line of the house. If a stairway angles to a landing it will help to slow the downward energy before it picks up again. Spiral staircases create the most disturbances, especially when they are in the center of the house. Spiral staircases that are nested off to the side and spiral down to a landing are acceptable. Stairways that are steep are never good, as with anything in the house you should never feel unsafe. Stairs that don't have risers (a riser is the vertical part of the stair) will also feel unsafe and are to be remedied or avoided. When the stairway is open and spacious the energy has a chance to disperse and won't have as much of a descending force. A stairway that is in *direct alignment with any exterior door* will create an energy leak for the house. Most floor plans have plenty of space to arrange furniture, plants or decorative room dividers to contain the energy from traveling down the stairs and out the door. Also be careful if a stairway opposes the door of a bedroom, it may create pressures in the life of the person who sleeps in the room.

Stairways continued

In some cases there are exceptions to the stairway configurations that have been described. Stairways that face the direction of the front door but are offset a bit will have less of a problematic effect. Some stairways may face the front door but there is a spacious foyer between the front door and stairs. It's even better if the foyer is rounded, this will soften the energy from moving in a straight line towards the front door.

Split level floor plans pose a challenge for creating balance in your life. A person could experience life as very up and down. The "watery" movement of the split levels stairs may create more emotional ups and downs.

The main floor is seen as the "present". The second floor represents the "future" and a room, floor or basement that is *below* the main level is seen as the "past" (always use feng shui adjustments to correct this level). The inside of a single story or ranch style house is seen as the "present", while the front of the house represents the "future."

Finally, stairways should be well lit and designed so that whether you are descending or ascending it can be done with ease.

Application

The key to a split level floor plan is to use a subtle design concept to **unite the split levels**. Artfully carrying a theme, color or texture throughout the entire living space to unify the disparate areas will transform a floor plan that would otherwise have little harmonious flow to it. In some cases, a floor plan can be very problematic because of additions and remodeling that had a singular focus without considering the effect on the flow of the "whole" house. Where this is the case all the attention should be placed on a design concept that can remedy it.

Application

Ascending a flight of stairs can be made easier when there is something to draw your eye upward. Upward lighting and a beautiful painting at the top of the stairs will help to energize the climb. If there is a landing, avoid the temptation to put anything on the floor, it could create an obstacle or worse a hazard.

When the front door and the back door are aligned the *energy* (**feng shui concept #4**) coming in the front door quickly leaks out the back door. Unlike a stairway that faces the front door pushing energy out, a front and back door in alignment funnel energy right through the house. Recall that we are aiming for the "meandering stream" effect. Of course, there are many floor plans where the entrance is *wide and open* and the flow of energy is much more dispersed in different directions and not traveling in a direct line. Also, if the entrance hall and the space between the front and back door are spacious enough, furniture placement, decorative floor screens, potted trees and objects of art can be used to create the "meandering stream" effect. Redirecting and or containing the escaping energy can easily be accomplished with good feng shui placement. The best test to see if the front and back door are a problem is to notice where your attention goes. If you are inclined to walk directly to the back door you have a problem!

Feng Shui Concept #7

Energy leaks in a house can come in many different forms. It can be something obvious, such as; a leaky faucet or plumbing, windows and doors that don't shut properly, sprinkler run off, septic tanks that are poorly located, pool and spa equipment and other inefficiencies around the property.

Energy leaks can also be more subtle, like too many doors (especially glass) or windows, sky lights, bathrooms, wet bars and utility sinks to name a few. Large floor to ceiling mirrors facing windows or exterior glass doors will push energy out as well. All these features and extra conveniences should be well planned to minimize the draining of energy from a property.

One of the essential objectives of feng shui is to create a space that *contains the energy*.

A **bathroom/powder room located too close to the front door** will challenge the auspicious energy that is cultivated at the front door and entrance hall. In feng shui, bathrooms are considered as one of the big energy drains in the house. When they are located too close to the front door, the occupants of the house may have challenges with their health and money.

How close is too close? If the floor plan is such that you notice the bathroom when you enter the house it is not good. Some powder rooms are located just off the foyer but because of good design they have a low profile and you are not aware of its proximity.

Bathrooms

In feng shui there are so many things written about bathrooms and their dreadful influence on a house. What is all the fuss about? It primarily relates to yin and yang theory. (see the appendix for a complete discussion on Yin Yang theory.) **Bathrooms are seen as being too 'yin' along with constantly draining and flushing energy.** This is quite the opposite of the desired *'tight container'* that we have previously discussed. Yin is the cold, dark and still energy that, in the extreme, is associated with death. Yang is the opposite, being characterized by heat, brightness and vitality, the energy of the living. In feng shui we seek to minimize the yin influence of the bathroom on the house.

Bathrooms continued

Let me first give you the bathroom locations that are undesirable. As we discussed earlier, a bathroom located in close proximity to the front door should be avoided as well as a bathroom that shares a wall opposite the head of a bed or opposite the kitchen stove. In both of these cases there could be an impact on the health of the person or family. Bathrooms in the center of the house can create a continual disturbance. You should not be able to see the bathroom from the kitchen and eating area! Bathrooms that are accessed through bedrooms should 'feel' separate from the bed and sleeping area. In this case, the more space the better and I don't just mean separated by a wall. It is best if the bed is at least ten feet from the actual toilet. When a bathroom door and a bedroom door face one another-in other words if you walk out of the bedroom and walk directly into the bathroom, this is not good. The bedroom will constantly be influenced by the bathroom's draining energy.

Ideal bathroom design is where the toilet is enclosed (WC), separate from the rest of the bathroom and dressing area. If the toilet is hidden by a wall so that you don't see it when you walk in the bathroom this is also good. I realize most bathrooms are not designed with feng shui in mind so it is a good practice to close the toilet lid and keep the bathroom door closed when it is practical.

Bathrooms can have an influence on health as well as the 'life aspiration' related to the compass direction where the bathroom is located.

Application

Extra care must be taken to keep bathrooms well lighted and colorfully decorated. This will counterbalance the downward effect of the drains and the flushing of the toilet. Bright stimulating lights, colors that enliven and pictures that depict upward movement can all be used to adjust the energy of the bathroom. A sequence of three pictures can be hung to *step upward*, drawing the eye up. A decorative shelf or hand towel rack can be mounted a bit higher to create the same upward feeling. Mirrored or reflective crown molding can be installed to draw the eye upward an offset the draining effect in a bathroom. You can also replace the hinges on bathroom doors with ones that naturally close on their own. If the bathroom is in a high profile location, or in one you find undesirable, take all the necessary measures needed.

I think that some of the problems with bathrooms are a result of not paying enough attention to design and décor. Never allow a bathroom to get into disrepair, it will only add to the downward, draining effect If you keep bathrooms well maintained and cheerfully decorated they will not have a negative impact on the house.

Also, take into consideration that the bathroom dressing area is where we begin preparing for the day. From a psychological point of view, you want to begin your day in a space that is cheerful and energizing.

When **the bedroom is too close to the front door,** or more specifically when you can see the bed from the front door, it will have an influence on a person's motivation. Many people enter their house from the garage, but in cases where the front door is the primary entrance, *seeing their bedroom when they first enter the house* will send an unconscious message of "rest" to the brain.

When the **kitchen is too close to the front door,** food will be a big focus for the household. I have seen this express itself in different ways from the positive to the negative. I myself once lived in a house where the kitchen and dining room were close to the front door. In less than 2 years I felt compelled to study professional culinary art and people were always eating at my house. I also became rather obsessed with films that had food as a major theme in the movie. With all the wonderful culinary experiences in that house, my family and friends would not have considered the effect of the kitchen and dining room being near the front door as a negative. Looking back, I can see the imbalance of energy expressing itself too much in a single direction. On a more serious note, people can be challenged by the location of the kitchen and the front door, especially if they already have problems with eating disorders or other health related imbalances.

Now, that we've discussed the top 5 challenges in detail let us turn our attention to rest of the house.

Leaving the entrance hall

The next thing I look for in an entry way is to notice what direction I feel compelled to walk towards, once I leave the entrance hall. This is a good way to measure how evenly the energy in a home disperses and flows. Some floor plans will strongly *funnel* the energy in one direction. This may be due to the architecture or the décor; sometimes it is a combination of both. As an example, after leaving the foyer you may be pulled to the rear of the house by a back door in line with the front door or a view of the city or ocean. In this case, objects of art or a decorative piece of furniture can be strategically placed to slow and modify the flow of energy. Another example is a split-level with descending stairs that quickly draws you into another part of the house. If the energy settles nicely in the foyer, it will easily disperse in different directions and carry on throughout the rest of the house. This is the best indicator for determining the natural energy flow of the house. Some houses don't offer a choice; you have to move only in one direction, and that's alright, just pay attention to where that is.

Application

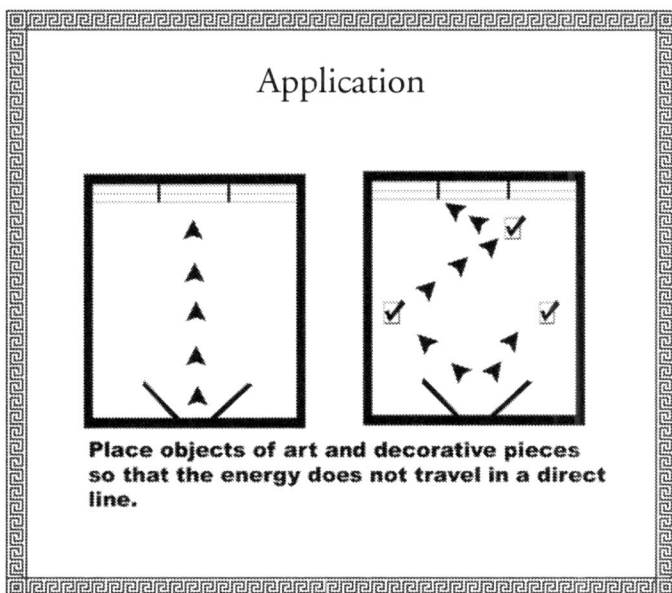

Place objects of art and decorative pieces so that the energy does not travel in a direct line.

火 水 木 土 金

7. – Key Areas in a Home

Rooms with the Greatest Influence

The entrance hall or "room of first impression" has a tremendous impact on the feng shui energetically and psychologically. Once set, the particular tone and atmosphere will be carried throughout the home.

The master bedroom and then the kitchen follow in their significance as important feng shui factors in a home. Each of these will be covered separately for their meaning and significance.

The appropriate design and usage of rooms will add to the overall balance of a home. Understanding the characteristics of yin and yang will help you make suitable design and color choices for a particular room. For example, the family room and living room where people gather should naturally lend itself to a higher level of energy (yang). Whereas a den, study or home office might be lesser yang, enabling a person to focus but not feel fatigue. A dining room will be a relaxed setting that enables people to eat and converse in manner that is conducive to good digestion. Avoid artwork or color that may be over stimulating in the dining room. In Taoist thought one never discusses illness or health matters while eating! The bedrooms should primarily have a yin, restful quality to them and I will discuss how to achieve that in the section on bedrooms.

Center Area

In feng shui, the 'center' of the home is referred to as "heaven's heart"; it is that important hub, around which everything centers. Earth is the element associated with the center. When the center is solid and stable like the earth, then the rest of the home will be also. A staircase or a bathroom located in the 'center' of the home is seen as creating too much movement for an area that should be still, solid and steady. If a part of the center section of your home is missing take the necessary steps to fill it in. Create an outdoor setting that feels like a natural extension of the house. (See house shapes) Utilize a hardscape design, oversized ceramic pots, cement pillars, umbrellas, out door rugs and furniture. Even though the roof may be missing at least you will have improved an important area of the home.

Application

To enhance the 'center' area of the home, place an object of art that has a heavy solid quality to it. Artwork depicting rolling hills (no water) and the color red will add to the solid earth element of the center. Take special care to place something that you really enjoy looking at and has special significance to you. The piece should symbolize health, vitality and balance.

The Garage

If the garage is attached to the house it is considered part of the home. We consider all of the rooms that are under the same roof as part of the whole. If you enter the house through the garage the single most important thing is that you are able to easily get into your house from your car. Having to step over or duck under *obstacles* in your path day after day is a frustrating message to send to your unconscious mind. You don't want your environment to reinforce the idea that life is full of obstacles and annoyances! If your garage is not finished take some steps to make the garage more organized, attractive and pleasant. Hang some nature themed posters or anything that brightens the space. Hazardous and toxic materials should be contained in one area or taken to an appropriate disposal site. Whatever condition the garage is in will affect the rest of the home.

Note: If you have rooms that are rarely used it is nice to periodically open the doors and windows to refresh that part of the home.

Clutter

Eliminating clutter is the first step in the feng shui process. If you have a lot of accumulation, all of your focus should be on eliminating and organizing your environment.

Clutter Continued

Energy does not flow well in a crowded space and the lack of circulation may have an impact on your health. I have never been in an overly cluttered environment where the person's health was optimum. It certainly sends the psychological message that your life is overwhelming and unmanageable. Be sure to include the side and backyard as well as the garage. Do your best to clear your property of clutter so that you can open up space for new opportunities. If you have a lot of accumulation it is a good idea to set some criteria before you begin the process of clearing.

I simply encourage people who have difficulty letting go of things to ask, **"Does this item reflect or express who I am now, or where I am going in the future?"**

Do not underestimate the power of divesting yourself and your living space of accumulation.

"Have nothing in your houses that you do not know to be useful, or believe to be beautiful."

—William Morris

Feng Shui Concept #8

The **commanding position**, as it is called in feng shui, is a location that has an optimal view and command of the space with strong support in the back. This criteria, is used for bed and desk placement in a room or an office. The concept of the **commanding position** is also applied to the *location* of the master bedroom as well as the office's of managers and chief officers.

Whether you are in your bed or sitting at your desk the door should never be behind you. Ideally, there should be a solid wall behind your headboard or in the case of an office, the chair where you sit. The 'solid wall' provides the *mountain form* that you learned about in **Feng Shui Concept #1**. Psychologically, this positioning provides security, support and protection, especially when you are sleeping. When the door is behind you, out of view, it puts your body on alert, whether you are aware of it or not.

In order to have full *command* of the home, it is best if the master bedroom is in the rear. Likewise, a business owner or an officer in a company will benefit from having an office location in the rear, away from the front door. The **commanding position**, naturally lends itself to supervision and administration.

Bedrooms

The bedroom is an important feng shui factor. I've come to understand the sleeping area as subtly *formative*. Perhaps it's the influence of Jungian dream analysis which views the archetype of the bedroom as the inner most recesses of our consciousness. While on consultation, I've seen the unfortunate correlation of a troubled marriage and the condition of the master bedroom. I've observed that the personal space of the bedroom can be reflective of a person's inner life and present life circumstances.

Family dynamics and the appropriate bedroom

The harmony and balance of family relationships can be supported by the bedroom location. If you apply **feng shui concept #8** then the optimum location for the parent's bedroom is in the rear of the home. The **commanding position** of the master bedroom will naturally support the parent's authority in the home and children will feel more secure. When this is not the case and the children's bedrooms are in the rear there is often a power struggle going on. The parents are trying to maintain their authority and the children feel empowered by the commanding location. This same concept can be applied to an owner of a house who has roommates. If the owner of a home has roommates, the owner should always have a bedroom in the commanding position, this will ensure that her roommate agreements will be met. Be aware that it is more difficult to get a roommate or visitor to leave when they are rooted in the rear of the home.

Younger children will naturally feel more secure when their bedrooms are closer to their parents and further away from the front entrance. Whereas teenagers, who are preparing to go out in the world, will more appropriately have a bedroom closer to the front of the home.

Bedrooms over the garage

Bedrooms located over the garage are essentially unstable and very difficult to balance because of the movement of the cars and the opening and closing of the garage door. The exhaust and gas fumes tend to permeate the floor as well. Such rooms are more suitable as bonus rooms, guest rooms or an office.

Electronics and Overcrowding

In earlier times, bedrooms were primarily for sleep, now they are multifunctional, especially for children and teenagers.

Generally speaking, children aren't troubled by sleeplessness like adults, so having a 'busy' room for a young person usually isn't a problem. I don't recommend having computers, exercise equipment or any reminders of the office in adult bedrooms.

Application

Alarm clocks and other **electronics** should be kept at least an **arms distance** away from your head when you are in bed. Baby monitors tend to give off high electromagnetic fields, so take care not to place them under the crib. Electric blankets expose your body to a continual electrical current that may affect your health in general.

One of the big mistakes I see in bedrooms is over crowding with furniture. It is usually that 'one' extra piece of furniture that bogs down the energy in the room and sets the room off balance. When we remove that 'one' piece, the entire room opens up. Pay attention to where you may have exceeded the furniture limit in the bedroom. Energy doesn't move well in an overcrowded room and that can be unhealthy, particularly in a bedroom.

Tall shelves should be located as far away from the bed as possible and well anchored. Furniture should never be placed so that it is towering over the bed, particularly near the head of the bed. Large paintings with heavy frames should not be hung over the head of the bed. If the wall needs something, textiles are the most appropriate to hang above the headboard.

Color

The three colors that are the most unsuitable for the bedroom are red, blue and purple. Red is too stimulating a color for a bedroom when you are trying to achieve the restful 'yin' quality. Too much red in an environment will create restriction, aggravation and in the extreme, anger. The color blue is calming and soothing but being surrounded by blue walls can give a person "the blues" and be depressive. The color purple is interesting because it is associated with the metaphysical and spiritual side of life. It is associated with the robes of priests and royalty. It has a quality of separation from the world and in the extreme, separation from life on this earth. As you can see all colors have a dualistic quality to them and care should be taken when painting the bedroom.

Bed Positioning

The area where the bed is and how the bed is positioned in the room must be conducive for restful sleep. Placing the bed in the **commanding position** will be the first priority. Some rooms can be challenging because of the configuration of the door, windows and closet. The two main things to remember are: a view of the door and a solid wall behind the headboard. Try to avoid positioning a bed under a window. Small portal designs are fine but know that the larger the window the more external influences are present and this can disturb the sleep. While in the sleep state the head feels overly exposed, which can be interpreted on a subtle level as lacking security and support. Ensure that the wall where you place the head of the bed is not adjoined to the kitchen's appliances, the bathroom's toilet or the family room's entertainment center. Additionally, inspect the exterior wall of the headboard location for circuit boxes, air conditioning units or any other energy emitting utilities. Finally, never place a bed with the feet pointing out the door. This is alarmingly called "the coffin position", as in carrying you out feet first!

Beds

The optimum bed design is a wooden frame, with a headboard made of solid wood. A solid wood headboard provides strength and support much like the "mountain form" at the rear of the house.

The following are some **bed designs** that can be problematic and the reasons why:

Sleigh beds, because of the curved headboard, can never be positioned flush with a solid wall. The foot boards are seen as cutting off and hindering your feet, consequently your ability to be successful in the world is challenged.

Beds made of metal are more susceptible to electromagnetic fields in the room and their headboards are usually designed with bars or slats creating a 'cage' like effect.

Bunk beds are a great space saver and seem like the only solution for some families, but I don't recommend them. The upper bunk and certainly not the lower bunk have enough clearance above. Children may find them fun and adapt to them but the design is claustrophobic and confining. I had one client who kept asking me if there was any feng shui that could improve the bunk bed. I told him there wasn't; later he revealed to me that his son didn't like sleeping in his bed and his asthma was worsening.

Beds Continued

If you have a headboard with shelves it would be best to replace it with a solid wooden headboard. In the meantime, avoid keeping a lot of clutter near your head. If the shelves are mirrored, use some fabric or pillows to cover the mirror.

Application

If a teenager's (15+) bed is against the wall, you might suggest moving it so that there is space to walk on both sides. This will help social development and confidence building. Younger children may feel more secure next to the wall and that's appropriate.

Application

The commanding position layout can be applied to the home office or study area to increase focus and productivity. I can always tell how conducive a work or study space is by the position of the furniture. People don't work well with their backs to the door and will unconsciously struggle and procrastinate on their tasks. In order to take advantage of the commanding position in an office, you will have to float your desk so that you can sit with the supportive wall behind you and the door in full view.

Master Bedroom

The master bedroom is one of the key areas for the home owner. A **square** master bedroom is ideal because this signifies the **stability of the earth**. When a square is in the middle of a circle it is symbolic of the earth (square) being encircled by heaven (circle). This arrangement was used in the design of the ancient Chinese coins which have a hollowed out square in the middle. Each dynasty had a coin specifically designed for the ruling Emperor. In ancient China, feng shui masters served as advisers to the Emperor on political affairs, military strategies and were also charged with designing an auspicious coin for the Emperor's dynasty.

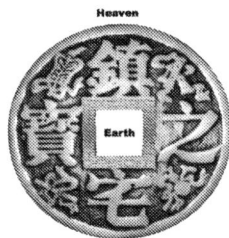

When a person is in their bed, they are supported by the earth (square room) which *naturally attracts* the circle of heaven.

This arrangement completes the trinity of heaven, earth and humankind.

Keep in mind all of the previous bedroom criteria; the commanding position of the bedroom and the bed placement, the bedroom should be decorated with a yin restful quality in mind, electronics should be kept to a minimum and a good distance from the sleeping area. This formative sanctuary should be cheerful, restful and evoke inspiration for you.

Once the bed is in the commanding position make sure that there is equal space on either side of the bed. Both partners should be able to easily access their side of the bed. This is crucial for a harmonious equitable relationship. If one partner has more difficulty accessing their side of the bed, it can lead to power struggles in their personal and business relationships. Matching night stands will further add to the sense of balance and strength of the sleeping area.

In general, fireplaces in the bedroom are seen as creating too much heat, in the way of anger and not passion. On a day-to-day basis, most people who have fireplaces in their bedrooms rarely use them. It is more typical to use them in vacation homes; just be aware of the potential for agitation and arguments as it relates to the bedroom space.

The following diagram depicts one of the weakest master bedroom layouts. I have seen many cases where this layout correlates with relationship problems and financial loss.

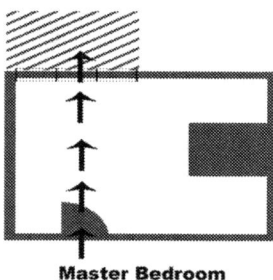

Master Bedroom

The Feng Shui Factor

When the master bedroom's door *aligns* with an exterior door to a patio or deck there will be major energy leaks and problems can occur. Smaller rooms will be more susceptible to this than larger master suites where the distance between the doors is greater. This can be somewhat minimized by strategic placement of furniture if the room is large enough, but it is never optimal.

Exterior doors in master bedrooms can tend to lead to one partner being away from home more. An exterior door that leads to a deck on the second floor will have less of an impact than when the exterior door is on the ground floor leading to a patio. I had a situation where one party had a metal stair case built onto the bedroom deck (to access the hot tub below) and within months one party had moved out and taken an apartment closer to the business. In this case, the bedroom door was aligned with the exterior door leading to a rear deck.

Application

Master suites typically have at least one exterior door leading to a deck or patio. Be aware of the door alignments as depicted in the diagram above; these are the most problematic. Window treatments, shutters and furniture placement can all be very effective in these situations. The key is to contain the energy of the bedroom with careful placement of furniture and décor so that it doesn't leak out.

Application Continued

If you've had relationship, health or financial challenges, one of the factors may be the energy leaks in the bedroom. As an example, I've seen sets of French doors in the master suite and the couple really struggling in several areas of their life. I am not suggesting that the exterior doors caused the problems but they certainly added to the instability. Imbalance usually attracts more imbalance and weakness. In cases like this the best feng shui remedy would be to replace the French doors with windows.

The best location for exterior access from a master bedroom is when the door is located in a recess, bathroom or dressing area just "out of sight" from the main bedroom area.

Mirrors in Feng Shui

The use of mirrors in feng shui is primarily associated with the Buddhist school of feng shui known as the 'Black Hat' founded by Professor Lin Yun. In this school of feng shui, mirrors are used as a tool to push out or deflect energy, draw it in, enliven a space, cool down the fire element as above a fire place, double, enlarge or invert an object or image and provide a rear view of a door when the commanding position cannot be achieved and your back is to a door.

Mirrors Continued

Avoid placing a mirror in your entrance hall facing the front door. In essence you will be pushing energy out the front door. This can also be true of mirrors facing other doors leading to the outside. Never hang a mirror so that it cuts off the head of the tallest person in the home. Mirrors with a lot of beveling or mosaic design can greatly skew the energy in a room. Blemished, flecked and warped mirrors will also distort personal image. Mirrors facing the bed can disturb the sleep by either making the energy in the room too busy or creating pressure by concentrating an excess energy on the sleeping area. This can certainly be the case with floor to ceiling mirrored wardrobe doors.

If you follow these guidelines when placing mirrors*, the balance in your home will not be affected.

The Kitchen

The kitchen is considered a key area of influence in feng shui. The preparation of meals and the nutrition we take into our bodies affect our **health** and well-being. The mood of the cook and the atmosphere of the kitchen are the unseen ingredients in your food. The stove is seen as an active generator of wealth, **abundance** and a successful career. The kitchen is the area of the home where all 5 elements (water, fire, wood, earth

* See Appendix D for Bagua Mirrors

and metal) join and interact. The interaction of the elements, especially fire and water can affect **harmony** and cooperation among family members.

The Stove

In feng shui, the stove is considered a significant focal point of importance; it is something to be cared for and protected. It should never be in the direct path of a door way or positioned so that the burners are overly exposed to cross drafts from windows. Gas ranges with multiple burners (5+) are considered to be the most auspicious. Cooking with real fire is understood to stimulate abundance and add the fire element to the energy of the food as opposed to electrical or microwave. There should be ample clearance above the burners, designs that have an oven or microwave above the range will suppress the fire energy. Hoods should be mounted to their specifications well above the burners. Of all the appliances the stove should be clean and in good working order.

When the sink and the stove are aligned directly opposite one another the water is in conflict with the fire element and may result in agitation and arguments. Having the sink and stove offset will minimize the controlling cycle of water over fire. It has become fashionable in newly designed kitchens to have a small faucet next to the range to make filling pots more convenient. This kind of layout will greatly weaken the feng shui of the stove!

Application

As a practice, keep the water faucet pointed away from the burners. If your stove is directly opposite the sink, place a live plant next to the sink or on the island between them. This will add to the harmony of the kitchen.

Another custom is to place a mirror or other reflective surface behind the stove to double the image of the burners and to enable the cook to see who's behind them (the cook needs a rear view mirror). In ancient China, woks were hung in this position to double the image of the stove and protect the cook.

Summary of the 3 Key Areas

My initial focus during a consultation is on the front entrance, master bedroom and the kitchen layout. As it relates to the interior, I have found that these areas have the greatest impact. I evaluate the entrance hall to ensure that none of the **top 5 challenges** are weakening the feng shui. While touring the home the master bedroom is examined for commanding location, layout, decor, and the bed position. During the assessment of the kitchen, the location of the stove is checked and I make sure the client understands the concepts and practices for the kitchen as it relates to the stove area. These key areas are thoroughly examined to ensure the most favorable feng shui conditions are present. I feel assured when these areas are strong the client will have sufficient support to improve and enhance any area of their life in the future. It is important to note that when these favorable conditions exist, it is less likely that the environment will be competing with the personal energy of the client.

8. – Interior Pathways & Design Features

Connecting the Rooms

The hallways that connect the rooms will be a significant feng shui factor in the overall flow and natural traffic patterns in a home. The hallways are the interior energy channels and the doors are the vital entry point for energy to flow into a room.

Doors

The entrance to a bedroom or office can be viewed as an important microcosm of the house or building. Apply the same guidelines to the room's entry point that we discussed for the front door entrance of the home.

Application

Consider the entry door to a bedroom or office as a stepped down version (microcosm) of the entrance to a house. Ensure that the path to the door is unobstructed by furniture or clutter of any kind either in front or behind the door. A large armoire or book case in close proximity to the door will over power the entry point for that room and inhibit the flow of energy. The door to the room must be able to completely open; avoid placing anything behind the door that will impede its opening.

If a room has two doors of entry it is best to choose one for the entrance to the room. This will ensure that the feng shui of the bedroom or office will be optimum.

Also, doors that are never used should never be noticeably barricaded. Sometimes, when a door is never used things get placed in front of it but the door is still visible. Inventiveness and creativity will have to be employed to make the second door or the door that's never used disappear. This may be a good location for an oversized bookcase or armoire. Shades, textiles, fabrics and of course removing the door are some suggestions.

A general feng shui guideline is to remove all obstacles from passage ways so that nothing is impeding the natural flow of energy.

Hallways

Long hallways tend to accelerate energy comparable to an alleyway between two buildings; the rush of energy is not as apparent in a home but the forcefulness of the energy is similar. The door of a bedroom or office that faces the end of a long hallway will be in a situation just like a house at the end of a "T" intersection on a street. Forceful energy focused on the door of a bedroom or office will weaken the feng shui of that room. The occupant of a bedroom with a weakened entrance may be susceptible to some type of energy imbalance.

Energy Imbalances

How do energy imbalances in the environment express themselves in our lives? First of all, energy imbalances manifest themselves differently for each individual. They exhibit themselves in areas where weakness and susceptibility already exist in a person's life, such as health, relationships, finances, and self esteem to name a few. In other words, people can typically find a theme when it comes to their challenges in life. The interesting thing about feng shui is that the living space will often reflect where a person's challenges may be.

The key is to use your feng shui knowledge to strengthen the areas that are weak so that over time you can see improvement. With some good investigative work, you may be able to correlate the imbalances in your living space to the areas of your life that you find challenging. Understand that correcting the feng shui will be one factor in improving a particular area of your life.

Changing your environment opens the door for improvement

Feng shui corrections can be a catalyst for improvement by compelling you to take some action toward change. As an example, someone will make changes in his or her living space with the intention of finding a companion. Specific feng shui placement is used to make the home inviting and welcoming for a new relationship. As a result of their intention and the action they take in their environment, they find themselves in a workshop about relationships, reading a book, or receiving advice and counsel that will better equip them for a healthy relationship. Life itself unfolds in ways that are unexpected and unpredictable. The results you get from feng shui will show up in various ways—trying to correlate a one to one relationship or cause and effect connection isn't always possible. Feng shui is one way you can create the means for your personal growth and the realization of your goals. It is really a function of what you **"intend to create" and then taking action**, by literally setting the stage through the means of your environment.

Application

Finding ways to **soften the direct flow of energy in a long hallway** can be challenging. Decorative and ornamental molding can be used to create an archway or other architectural affect in the hallway, thereby slowing down the direct flow of energy. Where space allows, strategically hang artwork to encourage the energy to meander like a stream rather than move in a direct line. Any reflective or shiny object of art carefully placed will attract the otherwise straight moving energy to itself. In this case, you can mount a small decorative ledge midway in the hall and place a reflective object of art on it. Hanging a faceted crystal will also help to disperse and slow down the energy.

Additionally, steps should be taken to strengthen a bedroom or office **door at the end of the hallway.** Place something reflective above the door itself or at eye level. A decorative metal door ornament used for a front door can be used for this purpose with the exception of a lion or other animal icon.

Hallway and door configuration influence the harmony of people in a home. The tripling of doors on both sides of a hallway can agitate relations among people. Multiple doors in a long hallway can instigate competition because each door is seen as competing for position. When doors are positioned directly across from one another there will be constant opposition. The opposing doors want to consume the other and this can add to sibling rivalry and other discord.

Application

Aside from physically changing the doors to off-set them, the only way to correct opposing doors is to create a diversion or separation between the doors. **Make a distinction between the doors** by mounting something ornamental on the sides of the door or above it to distract the competing doorways. Hanging a crystal or light fixture from the ceiling to disperse and separate the energy between the two opposing doors is the most common way of correcting this problem.

When the opposing door to the bedroom or office is a bathroom door or an exterior door it will drain the energy from the room and weaken the feng shui. Take all necessary measures to diffuse and deflect the direct path between these two doors.

Pulling it all together

The **application** below is a must because it works on so many levels. It will help you **balance and unify the house** by making sure these strategic areas are not over looked.

Application

Analyzing the Traffic Patterns

With a copy of your floor plan in hand, walk the natural traffic pattern of your home. Notice which area or wall your eye is immediately drawn to as you turn a corner into a hallway or enter a room. Make a note on your floor plan which walls or areas these are. It is important to deliberately enhance the focal points in the traffic patterns. Make sure there are no blank walls and that the artwork in these key areas is inspiring to you. A blank wall in a strategic area sends a message of obstruction and uninspiring art work will undermine your enthusiasm. These key areas can have a great influence on your well being so be sure to use them well.

I encourage taking your floor plan and measurements with you when you shop for these areas so that you can make very specific purchases.

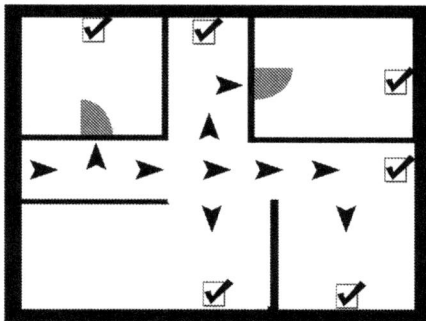

A Final Look at Traffic Patterns

The home's architecture, along with the placement of furnishings and decor will dictate the traffic patterns, which then become habituated by the occupants of the home. When the living space is rearranged the habit patterns will be disrupted and new ones will eventually emerge. You can apply this knowledge of traffic patterns and habits to areas of the home you want to improve. Clutter tends to accumulate in areas where the furnishings stay the same. By modifying these areas the habits and traffic patterns will be altered.

In some homes, there are rooms that are rarely used and it can be an interesting exercise to find ways to draw traffic into them. These habits and patterns are often noticed when entertaining, especially when guests assemble in the same area for the entire gathering. This is a good indicator for you to use your feng shui knowledge by asking, "How can I draw the energy (people) into other areas of the home?" What kind of placement will be required to accomplish this?

Remember, that you can change the way you respond to your living space by adding, removing or rearranging anything.

General Design and Architectural Features

Ceilings and Beams

The height and design of the ceiling will affect how the energy is dispersed in the room. Vaulted and high volume ceilings cause the energy to travel upwards leaving an energy vacuum in the room.

Application

If a room has high or vaulted ceilings, it is important to place some heavier solid pieces in the room to help anchor and stabilize the energy. Earth colors and accenting with darker shades will also help in balancing the tendency for the energy to rise with the high ceilings. Placing objects of art and having architectural features that are rounded will help balance rooms with high or vaulted ceilings.

When ceilings are overly angled and low slung, it compresses the energy in the room and the opposite strategy must be used.

Application

When a ceiling is low and angled, place potted trees (real or artificial) in the corners to give the impression of height, growth and expansion. Any object of art or painting that has a spacious, airy feel will offset the compressed feeling of a low angled ceiling. Mirrors will also open up a space that is affected by a low angled ceiling. Be careful to follow the mirror guidelines. Furniture should be minimal and the wall colors and décor should be light and airy.

Depending on the height and design, ceiling beams will tend to slice up the energy in a room and make it chaotic. In a sitting area people unconsciously tend to sit on either side of a beam. In feng shui, there is always a concern that a bed positioned under a beam will affect the part of the body where the beam crosses or that the edges of the beam will create a darting arrow affect.

Application

The best solution for an intrusive beam, especially in a **key area** (bedroom), is to wrap it with dry wall, bull nose the corners and paint it the color of the ceiling. Sometimes painting the beam the color of the ceiling will be sufficient but the edges may still be a problem. Another suggestion would be to creatively drape fabric to soften the beam's impact.

Skylights

Skylights are another debatable feng shui feature in a home. From a feng shui perspective, the two biggest concerns are the invasiveness of the construction when cutting into the roof, and creating an energy leak because the flow of energy will naturally travel upwards and out. It would be inadvisable to place a sky light in the bedroom over the bed. Placing skylights in other rooms in a home should be evaluated in relation to the number of exterior doors and windows that already exist. The aim for the interior space is to contain and preserve energy

Application

I have discovered that solar tubes are a great alternative to sky lights. They are much less invasive from a construction stand point and while letting the natural light in, the room is not thrown off balance by rising and escaping energy that is typical of a skylight. The round shape of the solar tube is subtle, making it more like a light fixture attached to the ceiling. All and all they are a great alternative to the skylight.

Poison Arrows

Bull nosed corners and arched doorways are wonderful features that add to a smooth fluid feel in a home. Many feng shui solutions can be found in a simple curve or circle. There is a saying in feng shui that says, "An ounce can move a thousand pounds." This means that the subtlest design feature or arrangement can alter an entire room.

Areas in the home where you spend a lot of time such as the bed, desk and any other areas should be examined for "poison arrows." There is an unconscious tendency to avoid areas where the energy isn't balanced. On a subtle level, there is an uncomfortable feeling; something that is not right but you can't quite put your finger on it. If darting energy is directed toward the bed, it may be difficult to relax. When the desk or study area is in the path of a poison arrow, fatigue and a lack of concentration may be the result. Check the areas of your home or office to see if there is an unnoticed poison arrow pointed in your direction.

Feng Shui Concept #9

The poison arrow in feng shui is anything that exists in the environment that sharply points or forces energy in one direction like a dart. The exterior of the home should be examined for neighboring construction (patios, protruding beams and roof overhangs) sending poison arrows toward key areas of your property. Examine doors, windows or any area where people congregate. I once had a brick fence built to house spa equipment and later realized the corner of the newly constructed fence was pointing directing at my back door. I placed a potted tree on rollers directly in front of the corner to absorb and minimize the affect.

The protruding beams make the entrance to this house very unwelcoming, and are a good example of exterior poison arrows.

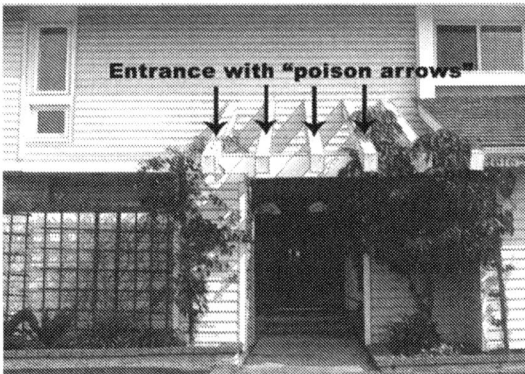

Entrance with "poison arrows"

Feng Shui Concept #9 - Continued

While in the interior space, **poison arrows** come from sharp edges and corners of walls, architectural features and furniture design.

The poison arrow has a two pronged affect, no pun intended. When you are sitting in the path of a **poison arrow** it puts the body under stress, which over time can be mentally and emotionally draining. Secondly, if your environment is poking and agitating you this may start to express itself in your interpersonal relationships as well.

Application

The best way to check your furniture placement for "**poison arrows**" is to position your self in the area and carefully scan the room. Look for corners and sharp edges from walls, columns, beams, tables, counters and other items or art work.

The key is to soften or deflect the poison arrow by placing something in front of the sharp corner. Some suggestions are a tree, plant, basket, a large ceramic vase, a rounded pedestal or other item. It is best to remedy these arrows when they are directed towards an area where you or your family gathers for extended periods of time.

Windows and Window Coverings

Simplicity is the best guideline for window design and window coverings. Too many bevels, etched glass and molded panes create distortion and your vision is always trying to correct, adjust and focus. In terms of balance, it is a strain for the eyes to continuously make these adjustments. Main windows should never be covered with mini or louvered blinds because your eyes will constantly be trying to correct their focus by searching for the light between the shades. It is best to completely draw the window coverings during the daytime for windows that are a main focal point in the room. Use window coverings that are easy on the eyes.

Application

It's a good practice to close your blinds when the sun has set. During the day time, the vitalizing yang energy has entered the house. By closing the blinds after dark, you are keeping the beneficial yang energy inside throughout the yin cycle of night time. This practice will help keep the energy of your home balanced and attuned to nature's rhythm.

Lighting

It is evident that throughout the holiday season the festive lighting has a tremendous effect on people's *moods and energy level*. Light fixtures and lamps that are **upward lit** will naturally elevate the atmosphere of the home. Conversely, lighting that is not well dispersed and directed downward casts shadows and lowers the energy of the room. Some feng shui experts do not like canned ceiling lights because of this. My concern with canned lights is not only how they light the room but the electromagnetic fields that are a by-product of the extensive wiring in the ceiling. I regularly detect higher EMF readings in homes that have a lot of canned lights. The most unsuitable light is cool white florescent light. It is known to cause headaches, eye strain, irritability and fatigue.

Application

Chandeliers, bowl pendants and upward lit wall sconces and lamps are the best designs to enhance the feng shui of a room. Crystal chandeliers will bring the most auspicious energy to the home, particularly when hung in the southwest part of the house.

Full spectrum lights are very helpful for people who are susceptible to "seasonal affective disorder" (SAD).

火 水 木 土 金

9. — The Five Elements

Living with Natural Materials

Densely populated cities, suburban sprawls and long distance commuting has effectively disconnected much of the population from nature. Most people who live in these areas have to make a concerted effort to spend time in a natural setting. Designing a living space with natural materials such as wood, stone and marble, and incorporating colors and artwork that reflect nature can help restore a connection with the natural world.

The Five Elements

Incorporating the five elements of **fire, earth, metal, water** and **wood** into your home's décor is a subtle but effective way to create an environment that is allied with natural law and cycles. Balancing the elements for the location and climate where you live, the architecture and lighting of the room and the compass direction will add another layer of feng shui attunement to your home. The five elements can be represented in your home by the actual element itself or its color and its shape.

Each of the elements has an energetic property that brings a particular quality into the home. People will often go through stages where they gravitate towards one element more than another because they are seeking the characteristics of that element. I had a client whose home had many beautiful objects of art made of metal and her personality certainly expressed what is known as metal traits. Some of the metal traits are independence, creative expression, assertiveness and communication. In this case, the excessive amount of metal in her home indicated that she was having some frustration with her creative expression. After our discussion she concluded that, by surrounding herself with so many objects of art made of metal, she was trying to bring about change in the areas of her life that correlated to the metal element. It is similar to having a nutritional deficiency where we crave specific foods in order to get the missing nutrients. You may get a clue about what qualities you are trying to bring into your environment if the décor has become dominated by one element rather than having a balanced complement of all the elements. Most art pieces and general décor have a mix of the five elements but sometimes one element can become dominant in an environment. This section of the book will help you analyze your living space from the viewpoint of the five elements.

The five element system may seem quite esoteric at first glance, but it is worthwhile to be able to identify each of the elements and what influence they have on your home.

The dynamic cycle of change

In Taoist thought, the five elements are understood to be in a dynamic cycle of transformation and change. Below is an example of the creative cycle of the five elements. In this representation each element gives birth to the next:

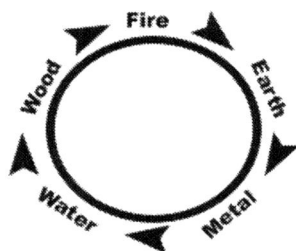

Each of the elements is associated with a compass direction, a season and climate. Additionally, in Chinese medicine the five elements correspond to the major organs in the body. Diagnoses and treatment of disease is achieved by balancing the interaction of the elements through nutrition, herbs, acupuncture and other modalities. The energetic qualities of the five elements are also related to specific character traits and emotional expression. In feng shui, we pay careful attention to how the five elements interact with one another. This interaction is described as producing, reducing, competing or destroying. For our purposes, we will focus on the **producing and reducing cycle** of the five elements. Each element has another element that produces it; this is referred to as the "parent." In the "parent" role, the element gives birth to, supports and enhances its "child" element. The opposite is true of the "child" element. When a particular element is in the presence of its "child", it will be reduced and distracted. If one element dominates the environment, you can introduce the "child" to reduce its influence. Conversely, the presence of the "parent" element will strengthen and enhance a weak or missing element. An example of this would be a home that is located near a body of water. By placing plants and trees (wood) between the home and the water, you can reduce the influence of water on the home if it is excessive. Wood is the "child" of water and water's natural tendency will be to move toward wood and be absorbed.

Let us now look at each element individually to better understand their characteristics.

Water - Connection

Water is represented in the environment by movement-shapes that are curvy and irregular, reflective surfaces, and the colors blue and black. The North compass direction, the winter season and cold climates are associated with the water element. It is known to be the strongest element and with its intensity and force, it can move around obstacles in nature and over time, erode mountains. In feng shui, water is associated with money, career, opportunities and networking. In the creative cycle, **metal produces water and wood reduces water**. In other words, if you have an excess of water in your environment, the placement of trees and plants will reduce water's influence. Conversely, the metal element will support and enhance water's presence when it is lacking. An environment that has too much water may feel emotionally unstable.

Water Element Furnishings

Fountains

Aquariums

Swimming pools

Hot tub

Ponds

Fresh standing water like a bird bath or bowl of water

Water can also be represented virtually with a pendulum clock, a metal windmill or any object that is in motion.

Application

The water element is associated with money and career so it is important to follow some basic feng shui guidelines for the placement of water features on your property or in your home. Waterfalls, fountains and other moving water should be gently incoming or cascading **toward the property or home.** Water whose direction is flowing away from the home is sending money and opportunities in the opposite direction from where you are.

If you are considering placing a permanent water feature, it is advisable to check the compatibility of the compass direction's element. For example, the fire element of the south or the mountain earth element of the northeast will not be suitable for a **permanent water** feature. If you are considering installing a large permanent water feature, it is best to consult with a knowledgeable practitioner to determine the most compatible location. Water features that move a considerable amount of water can make quite an impact on the home. Understanding which area of your home or property is suitable for moving water and which area needs stillness and solidity is another key factor to achieve a harmonious balance.

Wood - Growth

Wood is represented in the environment by plants, trees, pillars, columnar shapes and the colors green and brown. The East compass direction, the spring season and windy climates are associated with the wood element. The wood element's association with springtime will bring about new beginnings, growth and expansion. In feng shui, wood is associated with health, family unity and hospitality. In the creative cycle, **water produces wood and fire reduces wood**. An overly wooded environment can be rigid and inflexible lacking in fluidity.

Wood Element Furnishings

Vital lush foliage

Plants

Flowers

Trees

Floral patterns

Textiles

Tall wooden columns

In most circumstances, it is best to avoid cactus and pointy leaf plants.

Fire - Vitality

Fire is represented in the environment by heat, triangular, pyramidal shapes and the colors are red, burgundy and magenta. The south compass direction, the summer season and hot climates are associated with the fire element. The fire element will invigorate, energize and support physical vitality. In feng shui, fire is associated with fame, reputation, status and character. In the creative cycle, **wood produces fire and earth reduces fire**. An environment that has too much of the fire element will feel constricted and overly stimulated, making it difficult to relax.

Fire Element Furnishings

Lamps (upward lit)

Crystal chandelier

Fireplace

Fire pit

Barbeque

Red candles (Candles do not have to be burning—be safe.)

Triangular, pyramid shaped objects of art

Visual art depicting sunshine

Paintings with the intense colors of the sun or planets.

Earth - Stability

Earth is represented in the environment by that which is heavy, stabilizing and square in shape; the colors are yellow, gold and earth tones. The northeast (mountain) and the southwest (hill) are the compass directions. Earth represents the eighteen days between the seasons and the climate is damp. The earth element is solid, stabilizing and grounding, it is able to harness and hold energy in the environment. In feng shui earth is associated with knowledge, partnerships, balance and health. In the creative cycle, **fire produces earth and metal reduces earth**. Too much of the earth element in the living space will create inertia and sluggishness.

Earth Element Furnishings

Ceramic

Crystals

Porcelain

Heavy solid objects, trunks, low pedestals

Rocks

Ceramics

Earthenware

Metal - Change

Metal is represented in the environment by domes, arches and round shapes; the colors are white and grey. The west and northwest are the compass directions and the metal climate is dry. The metal element is a powerful dynamic force that can swiftly create change. In feng shui, metal is associated with creativity, benefactors and mentors. In the creative cycle, **earth produces metal and water reduces metal**. An overly metal environment will feel hollow and detached, making it difficult for people to relate. There may be a lot of talking but no real connection.

Metal Element Furnishings

Metal objects of art, sculptures and statues

Metal clocks with pendulums

Gongs

Dome shapes

Bells

Round metal plates and platters

Chimes

Coins

Metallic objects or paintings especially white and grey in color

Living in Harmony with the Five Elements

Application

Look for the influence of the elements in the décor, the shape of the home and in the climate of the region where you live. You can enhance the balance in your home by increasing an element that is missing or by reducing an element that is excessive.

When the "child element" is present, it will reduce the "parent element."

As an example, a home that has an excess of the earth element (stone, brick, earth tones), can be balanced by incorporating the metal element into the decor to reduce the heavy earth influence.

In a region that has a generally hot climate the cool dampness of the earth element, which is the child of fire, will help bring the heat into balance.

Waterfront homes are usually dominated by the water element and owners should be careful not to add more water by placing fountains or aquariums.

Owners of homes in regions that are heavily wooded and have longer rainy seasons can introduce the fire element to add warmth, brightness and balance to the excessive wood.

The key is to examine which elements are present and determine if any one element is overly dominate whether in the décor, architecture or the regional climate and seek to balance it.

Remember that the elements can be represented by the shape, color or actual element.

Competing Elements

When certain elements are paired in close proximity to one another, it can disturb the harmony in a home. Earlier we discussed the elements of fire and water as it relates to the kitchen sink and the position of the stove. Other pairs that are incompatible are **metal and wood, earth and wood, water and earth, fire and metal**. These mismatched pairs compete rather than complement each other.

Smaller accent pieces are less likely to have an impact but, large objects of art or a concentration of two of the mismatched pairs, fighting for the same space, can throw the balance of a room off. Look for metal objects of art placed next to trees or a concentration of house plants. A fountain near a fireplace or an outdoor fire pit is an example where elements will be competing rather than complimenting one another.

The Compass Directions

The compass directions and their association with the five elements is another area where you may **uncover pairs of competing elements**.

The **earth element** is associated with the Northeast and Southwest

The **metal element** is associated with the West and Northwest.

The **water element** is associated with the North.

The **wood element** is associated with the East and Southeast.

The **fire element** is associated with the South.

Application

By taking the **compass direction*** into consideration and looking for incompatibilities with the elements you may be able to further add to the harmony of your home.

If you have an excessive amount of the earth element in the North, you may want to replace it with objects of art that depict water and metal. You can remove, replace or follow the increasing and reducing guidelines to balance the five elements for each of the compass directions. If one area of the home feels out of balance or problematic, you may want to investigate whether the elements used in the décor are competing with the compass direction. If there is a concentration of house plants in the West and Northwest, that area of the home may be out of balance with the compass direction and influencing the harmony of the home. Imbalances won't be caused by accents and smaller objects of art; it's the larger dominant piece that you want to consider whether or not it is placed in a compatible direction. If the art in question is perfect for the spot but out of sync with the direction's element, consider changing it only if you think it's having an impact on the harmony of the elements. The feng shui knowledge is a tool to refine your environment not to make you unhappy about your favorite piece of art.

* See Appendix C

Stages and Layers of Feng Shui

Strong feng shui is achieved in stages and layers. The first and foundational layer is in the "form and shape" of the home which includes the neighborhood setting, the lot shape, the architecture and floor plan. The next layer is the design concept and decor which takes into account landscaping, the placement of furnishings, artwork, symbolism and the usage of color. Using the five elements in your choice of materials will fine-tune the feng shui in a subtle but powerful way adding another layer to the balance and harmony of your home. However you choose to apply the elemental approach, I encourage you to **balance the elements in your home with the climate and region where you live.**

火 水 木 土 金

10. – Feng Shui and Symbolism

Glass and Fragile Pieces

Glass has a breakable, fragile quality to it and is considered to be "breakable chi." Precious and delicate objects of art must always be secured and showcased in such a way so as not to create an uptight, nervous environment. Take steps to ensure that your environment is not permeated with anxiety because of art or furnishings that are fragile or inviting an accident. People don't realize how much nervousness can be infused into the atmosphere of a home concerning fragile pieces.

Potential Hazards

On an unconscious level, we take note of annoyances and hazards in the environment. They register just outside our conscious awareness and on a subtle level we understand that there is something present to avoid or adapt to. Your aim in feng shui is to create an environment that is free of obstacles, impediments and hazards so that you don't have to continually adjust your personal energy to your living space. That is why things that need to be repaired or replaced can be considered an improvement to the feng shui of your home. Additionally, by removing potential hazards you are also relieving the environment from an undertone of worry.

Thorny Plants

Pointy and prickly plants, such as cactus and other thorny succulents in the environment will register in the mind as dangerous and harmful. Avoid having these plants in areas where there is people traffic.

Application

Cactus and other pointy plants can be very useful to create a natural barrier, usually in particular areas on the perimeter of a property. It is best to utilize these plants as a way to keep things out as nothing sends a more clear message "to stay out", than a large thorny plant. Think of pointy and prickly vegetation as a natural shield and protection which can be utilized in specific areas of the property where needed.

Ceiling Fans

Ceiling fans have their pros and cons when it comes to the feng shui of a living space. On the favorable side, ceiling fans can reduce energy consumption by gently circulating air. They can also be a good solution for an area in the home where the energy tends to stagnate or feel stuffy. The chief concern with ceiling fans in feng shui is the chopping and chaotic effect the blades have when they are on a high speed. This can particularly be a concern when the ceiling fan is directly over the bed. If the fan is set on a high speed it will disturb the yin, restful quality of the bedroom and disturb the sleep. Another thing to consider is the inauspicious symbolism of sleeping directly under moving blades.

Weapon Displays

For feng shui purposes, swords and guns should never be hung on walls or displayed in the general living area. It is more appropriate to have weapon collections contained in a specific area outside the main house. Weapons in general signify "conflict", and when present may tend toward undermining harmony in relationships. Swords should always be in their sheaths and guns should be in a case.

Protective Icons

Statues such as lions, fu dogs, masks, totems, gargoyles and the like have a fierce protective quality to them. In various cultures, these icons represent protection from one's enemies; they are meant to gobble up, frighten and scare off menaces of all kinds. Often people will acquire these icons as art pieces while on travel and then inadvertently place them in areas that are inappropriate from a feng shui standpoint. It is best to position these pieces in locations on the perimeter of the home facing outward. To improve the feng shui avoid pointing them toward the interior of any gathering space or directly at your neighbor's front door.

Application

Chinese art is rich with symbolism and meaning, from the beautiful brush painted calligraphy to artifacts made of stone, wood, metal and textiles. The great artisans of the past intricately infused the icons, symbolism and imagery of their philosophy and culture into their art work. Feng shui enthusiasts have explored these symbols and adopted them for use to enhance their environments. **This type of feng shui placement is mostly effective because of the personal meaning the object has and the intention of the person using it.**

There are many feng shui books and websites that can instruct you on the meaning and usage of all the various icons and symbols. Some schools of feng shui employ their usage more than others. The feng shui factors that relate to the form, placement and flow of your home have a much greater influence than the usage of feng shui icons.

The following are some suggestions and guidelines for placing specific symbols:

The "**globe**" is a powerful symbol for **expansion, networking and recognition.**

A **pendulum clock**, as noted in the section on the 'water element', brings the virtual movement of water, but it can also be used to increase **motivation and productivity.** By coupling **time with movement** it will enhance the work or study area of the home or office.

Application Continued

Any picture depicting movement such as **horses galloping** or **ships sailing** should be hung so that the **movement is incoming rather than outgoing**. The image of galloping horses is used to stimulate opportunities; just make sure they are placed to gallop towards you. Of course, we are all familiar with the universal imagery and expression, "my ship has come in."

An antique **balanced scale with measured weights** can be placed near the center area of the home or on the middle level of a tri-level house to connect and balance the split levels. This denotes '**equilibrium in the center**', from which all things flow.

Make use of **current photographs** of family and friends on excursions and travel to inspire **future adventures**. Avoid placing photographs of the living on the fireplace mantel. **Maps** and travel books can also be used to stimulate travel particularly when placed in the northwest.

Photographs of children with their friends will help their social development and help foster healthy friendships. Dedicate a bulletin board or, even more energizing, buy a mobile that has clips to hold photographs.

Application Continued

Children can be motivated by the **sight of books** upon **entering the home** or when placed in one of the **strategic focal points**. This will help them stay connected to learning. The multi-tiered **"pagoda"** is used in study areas to signify academic achievement and motivate people to aspire to higher levels of development.

Enjoy your innovation and creativity as you experiment with symbols that are meaningful for you and then **place them with intention**. I have yet to meet an icon that has inherent magical powers. Although, if I found an amazing looking 'genie in a bottle' or 'a golden goose that laid golden eggs', I might buy it just to remind myself of what is possible.

The next section covers art in the environment and its general impact on the feng shui of the home as it relates to our psyche.

"Mind is creative, and conditions, environment, and all experiences in life are the result of our habitual or predominant mental attitude"

—Charles F. Haanel

Art - The Unconscious Messages

We are continually registering, processing and filtering the stimuli in our environment. Our internal response to artwork and what it symbolizes to us has a subtle but regular influence on our moods. It is very helpful to pay attention to how you respond to the themes, colors and textures of the artwork displayed in your home. The associations you make with the décor and artwork will trigger and reinforce a particular set of thoughts and feelings every time you see them (see **Analyzing the Traffic Patterns**). When you really give this some thought, you can understand the importance of this aspect of feng shui. The person who has a strong "visual" representation will be the most sensitive to this aspect of feng shui. It is important to realize that our thoughts create our feeling states.

There is a sequence to the interaction with the objects of art in our environment:

1. We see the art (visual representation).

2. We associate the art with "something" which stimulates thoughts.

3. Our thoughts then begin to produce our feelings about what the art symbolizes.

4. The result is a change in our state be it positive or negative.

This sequence happens so quickly that you are often completely unaware of it. What you may be aware of is some "residual feeling" from the art work but you haven't analyzed where the trigger came from. This powerful interaction is continually taking place in your living space and the good news is that you can use it to your advantage.

Let me reiterate at this time that clutter and the sight of unfinished projects will trigger a response, which is usually related to discontent, sense of overwhelm and unmanageability. The last thing we want from our environments is to *entrain* thoughts of overwhelm and unmanageability into our psyche.

Cases in Symbolism

The theme and message depicted in artwork is essential to feng shui. Artwork that evokes and elicits messages that strengthen and support your wellbeing will have the most positive impact on your living space.

1. On several occasions, I've had clients express difficulty in finding companionship. When I looked at the themes in their artwork, I found more than one picture depicting a lone isolated figure that sometimes hung in a very strategic area. A strategic area for partnerships is in the southwest and it is best to have "pairs" represented here rather than a lone figure. This would also make sense for the bedroom, the area of "family" (east), and the area of "helpful people" (northwest).

2. Another client had several medical instrument patents in frames hanging on the wall of their clinic. As it turned out, these patented instruments were unsuccessful as a business venture, perhaps because they were ahead of their time. I advised them to remove them for the time being because they were reminders of an untimely venture as well as the struggles they encountered seeking recognition for their work.

3. A business that I frequented had a highly unsuitable painting (for this type of business) hung in the commanding position of the owner's office. Over time, I observed the owner of this business become more identified with the themes in this painting than his own well-being. I knew when I saw the

painting in such a commanding position that he was making a "statement of identity" whether he was aware of it or not. Visual representations in the environment can reinforce habitual kinds of thinking whether beneficial or harmful.

Past, Present and Future

I believe that we are all wired differently when it comes to how we relate to the **past**, the **present** or the **future**. Some people are focused on the past more than the future and vice versa. Others are very much in the present without much thought for the future or the past. For most people their orientation is a mix of all three: **past, present and future.**

Application

Examine your living space to see how much of the "personal past" you are living with everyday. If you find that your environment is drawing most of your attention to the past ask yourself some questions. Does this make me happy, secure or content? Do I feel unsatisfied, frustrated or disappointed by what I see? For those who feel stagnate or "stuck in the past" you can use your feng shui placement as a remedy to bring you into the present.

It's best not to allow the past to be an anchor weighing you down. If you keep a collection of journals, letters, mementos and photos from the past, avoid storing them under your bed, particularly, mementos from past relationships or journals used as a cathartic tool.

Application Continued

At least once a year I go through my books and donate the ones with which I no longer have a connection because I have moved into new areas of learning. For years I have seen this as symbolically making space for new knowledge in my life and personal growth.

Whatever you determine about how much or how little of the past you want to live with, know that you can arrange your environment to reflect the present and include imagery that will help you shape your future.

火 水 木 土 金

11. – More Feng Shui Aspects to Consider

Compatible Environments

I sometimes encounter couples for whom the house is more supportive for one of the partners than the other. One of the individuals is experiencing a lot of success and satisfaction in their career, community life, health or creatively and the other partner seems to be struggling. In these cases, the compatibility of the home with the struggling partner may be a factor. Once again, I want to reiterate that the home's feng shui is one factor you can examine to determine how to make the home more supportive for the partner who needs it.

Let me give you a few examples and then give you some practical **application**.

As a consultant, you have to look at the history of a couple's experience in their home. How has your health, career, family life etc. been since living here? In one extreme case, one of the partners was having tremendous success and opportunities in her life while her partner was experiencing many financial set backs and over time began to have health issues. One of the main objectives for the consultation was to make the house more compatible and supportive for him.

When the individuals in a partnership are in very different places in their life it can also influence the selection of a home. One person feels good about themself, their career and family life while the other one is struggling. The home selection may reflect the exact state they are in and perhaps exacerbate the imbalance. This is why defining your goals and assessing your relationship with your partner will make a positive difference when selecting a home.

The often repeated phrase, "If you don't know where you are going, you will probably end up somewhere else", expresses the importance of defining your goals.

Application

In cases where one person feels out of sync and incompatible with the home one of the first priorities should be to focus on balancing the home for that individual. It may take some professional advice in order to pinpoint the best approach for accomplishing this. Start with these fundamental guidelines.

Balance the Feminine (yin) Areas

If the female needs support strengthen the southwest (matriarch) by enhancing the earth element (see Five Elements for guidance). The right side of the home (as you are facing outward toward the street) also relates to the feminine. The shape of the house and lot as well as the neighboring exterior structures and landscape should all be examined on the right hand side. Also look for pronounced irregularities in shape, overpowering structures or excessive draining.

Application Continued

Balance the Masculine (yang) Areas

If the male needs support strengthen the north-west (patriarch) by enhancing the **metal element**. The **left side** of the house as you are facing outward toward the street relates to the masculine. The shape of the house and lot as well as neighboring exterior structures and land-scape should all be examined on the **left hand side**. Also look for pronounced irregularities in shape, overpowering structures or excessive draining.

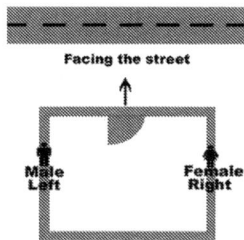

Assess the bedroom arrangement: bed place-ment, night stands and furniture for symmetry and balance. **Cramped or overcrowding on one side of the room will confine and restrict one partner more than the other.** In terms of male/female polarities and which side of the bed one chooses to sleep is a matter of preference. Also, look at pictures, symbolism, color and any décor that may be mismatched or inharmonious for one person more than the other. The picture below depicts a well balanced bedroom, no over-crowding, the position and scale of the furniture is balanced and equal for both partners.

The Feng Shui Factor

Application Continued

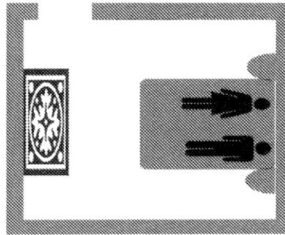

Use these guidelines to detect if there is a correlation between the partner and the areas that relate to him or her.

In general, the best circumstance is when both parties are in agreement and are enthusiastic about the feng shui enhancements or the features they are looking for in a home. As a consultant, the most successful consultations are those when the couple is in accord with one another-progress is made quickly and the desired outcomes are achieved more easily.

Feng shui and Life Circumstances

I am often reminded that the environment can mirror the current state of affairs in a person's life when I encounter a person who is coping with a difficult and challenging life circumstance.

I had a young client who purchased a home very soon after she had lost her husband. The curious thing was that her new home had very weak feng shui in the areas that relate to partnerships and marriage. No matter how you assessed the new home it was apparent that support for *relationships* was missing. My conclusion was that she was still in a place of grief and shock at the unexpected loss of her husband and the home reflected it. We discussed this openly and she felt confident that when the time came for her to deal with this aspect of her home she knew what adjustments to make in order to strengthen it for "partnerships". I've also observed a similar phenomenon with people who are looking for a home while they are going through a divorce. The houses they are attracted to somehow reflect their present feelings of instability and uncertainty.

Along this same theme I've had clients who have hit a rough patch or experienced a disappointment and it is reflected in their living space. During such times it is possible to make changes that end up weakening the feng shui. I asked a knowledgeable client why his bed was not in the **commanding position**. He told me it used to be in the commanding position but he moved it when he lost his job. Now that he was ready to move past his disappointment and feeling of disempowerment his environment began to reflect that.

The reason I write about these challenging life circumstances is to raise your awareness and encourage you take stock of where you are in life when making changes to your home or purchasing a home. Professionals in the health care field usually advise people who have gone through a difficult life event to wait as much as a year before making any big decisions about their life. Having said that, I am also sensitive to the fact that people don't always feel they have that option.

Understanding Space

Square Footage

Adequate square footage will have an influence on certain lifestyles. This is particularly true for people who tend toward right brain pursuits; those who meditate or are involved in creative endeavors often require a spacious environment in order to feel balanced. A good rule of thumb is a minimum of five hundred square feet per person.

Conversely, having too much square footage for too few people will create an imbalance. This is considered not having enough "people or living chi" to fill up the house. Family unity and a sense of connection between family members can be challenged when a home is too large. There is no specific ratio of people per square footage, it really depends on the family dynamics but too few people in a very large home will tend towards family members feeling isolated and disconnected.

Application

It is a good idea for someone living alone in a large home to periodically entertain, have house guests and host small gatherings to help balance the people to space ratio. Having a pet is also highly recommended to increase the "living chi" in the environment.

Feng Shui and the Foot Print of a House

The *occupants* **of large homes** are more **influenced by the exterior** forms, landscape and elements than smaller homes; this is due to the large footprint and higher profile of the house. The *occupants* **in smaller homes** will be less influenced by the exterior surroundings (smaller footprint) and more influenced by the interior forms, floor plan, arrangement and decor.

If you have a large home, the lot shape, the landscape and the surrounding structures are considered to be equally influential as the interior forms, floor plan and feng shui placement. While in a smaller dwelling the interior feng shui will be most important.

Compass Orientation

The classic feng shui model is a home that is situated with the back to the north and the front to the south. As we discussed earlier, this original orientation allowed the rear of the house along with the "mountain form" to support, protect and shield the house from the cold northern winds; whereas, the front *receptive* part of the home faces the warmth of the southern direction. It can be compared to the body where our back supports us and the front of the body is where we open to the world.

The various schools of feng shui are segmented based on their measurements and interpretations regarding the compass orientation. I encourage people not to become vexed over compass measurements. In the hierarchy of things a desirable compass orientation will not magically bring about good fortune if most of the feng shui essentials we have covered in this book have not been met.

Through observation and personal experience I have concluded that homes situated on a north south axis tend toward a smoother ride. This may be because of the natural magnetic poles of the earth. Other methods favor an east west orientation following the rising and setting of the sun. In the end, personal preference and climate will be the deciding factors. In a location where long snowy winters have to be considered, you will want the southern exposure to help melt the snow at the access points (front path, driveway) of the house. Any location where the weather can be extreme during the year the directional orientation will be an important factor to consider for the temperature differential.

火 水 木 土 金

12. – The Center Position High Profile Feng Shui

There are some excellent high profile examples that I want to present in order to deepen your understanding about feng shui. Ancient Chinese history offers the best context for understanding the center position of power. The ancient seat of power known as the "Forbidden City" is located in the middle of Beijing, China. For five centuries the Emperor and the royal families of China resided in the Inner Court of the City. In the Imperial Palace, the Emperor was like the sun, the center of the universe and everything was to revolve around the Emperor like the planets revolve around the sun. The royal color was yellow and it was forbidden for anyone else to wear the royal color.

Modern Power Moves

I personally, have no way of knowing whether feng shui was employed intentionally in the examples that follow but they do epitomize great feng shui form.

The first high profile example is Former President Ronald

Reagan's grave site at the Reagan library in Simi Valley California. When watching the broadcast of President Reagan's funeral I was astonished when I saw before me a modern day replica of an ancient Chinese burial site.

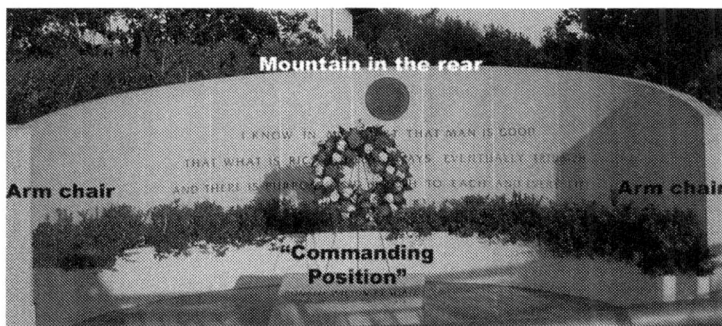

I later took this photo while visiting the library. In it, you can detect the perfect "arm chair" form surrounding and protecting the headstone that is **positioned in the center**, this along with the supportive mountain shape in the rear. The view from this site is one of a beautiful California landscape with views toward the west and northwest.

The second on my list was the remarkable layout of the stage and platform used at the 2004 Republican National Convention. All politics aside, when President George W. Bush walked beyond the traditional platform (no pun intended) to the "center" of the floor and positioned himself in the "middle" of the delegates, that was a classic feng shui power move. A stage and platform had never been designed like this before and while news media commentators were remarking about the unusual configuration, I was musing about how astute the Bush strategists were.

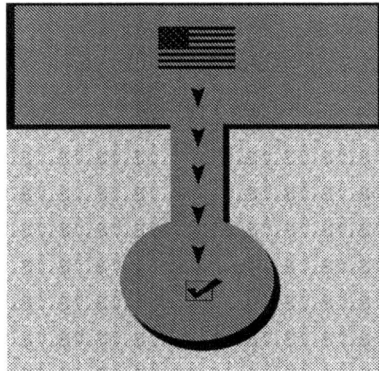

The Lakewood Church in Houston Texas is an extraordinary church in terms of the feng shui design. This successful church is the largest and fastest growing church in America, it has 42,000 visitors weekly. The stadium was formally the Compaq Center, home of the NBA Houston Rockets, a successful predecessor before Pastor Joel Osteen converted it into the Lakewood Church. It caught my attention because of the powerful feng shui form. It is a stadium bowl with concentric half circle seating, which strongly focuses all the energy on the stage. The symbolism used on the stage is also quite impressive. On one side of the stage is a large crystalline looking "globe" which is widely used in feng shui to signify worldwide fame and recognition among other things. Also noteworthy, is the symbol on the podium (Lakewood Church logo) which denotes "fire" (the fire element also correlates with fame and recognition) or perhaps in Christian terms "inspiration of the spirit". The shape and design of this church combined with the use of non-traditional symbols make this successful church a very interesting model for any organization that aspires to this kind of outreach. In an interview, I heard Osteen's wife say of her husband, "he makes everything he does look easy."

The television set in Harpo Studios where the Oprah Winfrey Show is taped underwent a metamorphosis a few years ago. This beautiful set looks very similar to the diagram below. Oprah does most of her interviews positioned nearer to the center, with her audience surrounding her. I don't know if they are intentionally creating these designs based on feng shui principles but they are excellent examples of feng shui form.

Successful cooking shows position their TV chefs in the center of a half circle cooking station to showcase their food. Years ago I attended a three day seminar where the principal presenter concluded the seminar from the center of the room.

The room was not set up for him to do this but somehow among more than 1,000 attendees, he pulled this off. He wanted the attendees to connect with him as the "authority" in his field of expertise.

I know a yoga instructor who places her mat in the center of the room to lead her class. She is a very popular instructor and I would not be surprised to hear of an offer for her own studio, an instructional DVD, or even a TV show. She brings a tremendous presence to her classes and distinguishes herself by positioning herself in the middle of her students.

Application

Take advantage of the "center position" arrangement when you set up a room for a presentation. I encourage my teacher/professor clients to arrange their classrooms with the desks and seating angled inward toward the instructor. This is a great help for teachers who need to establish their authority and create a central point of focus for their students. It will also discourage cross talk and other distracting elements. Take advantage of rooms where you have control over the seating arrangement. It is good feng shui strategy to plan ahead and have the seating and or tables arranged to these specifications. Additionally, make sure that you have some support for your back if possible. Make sure that your arrangement does not position you with your back to a door; a solid wall is best or improvise with some other supportive prop if necessary. Position yourself in the commanding position with the seating angled toward you.

Application Continued

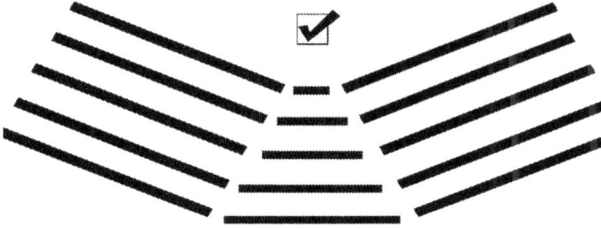

If you have a wall or a back drop behind you, place imagery that raises your profile. Be careful not to use something that distracts or detracts from you but rather enhances your influence and distinguishes you.

When these feng shui concepts are utilized for speaking engagements, workshops or any other presentations, it increases the attention, focus and connection with the audience as well as distinguishes and enhances the authority of the presenter. In simple terms, it makes your job easier.

火 水 木 土 金

13. – Better Designs

What would better designs look like? With a fundamental understanding of feng shui, home builders can design homes and plan neighborhoods that satisfy essential feng shui criteria and future home buyers will be more discriminating when selecting their homes:

✤ Green space or non-critical areas of a home can absorb the chaotic and hazardous energy of a T-intersection rather than a front door or other vulnerable areas of a home. Homes can be situated on a lot or designed in such a way so that the T-intersections have minimal or no impact on the home.

✤ Homes that must back to streets should have raised lots and higher fences to offset the instability that movement in the rear creates.

✤ Raised lots for homes built near busy streets will help minimize the noise and disturbance of the street traffic.

✤ Utilities should always be well planned so that poles and transformers do not encroach on the property.

✤ Entrances can be well designed for high visibility, and to be inviting and easily accessible. Stairways should never be located facing a front door or other exterior door.

✣ Floor plans can be designed so that entrances and exits are not aligned allowing energy to continually escape. Doors to rooms can be offset in hallways so that they are not located in *opposition* to one another.

✣ Home buyers will be more circumspect regarding developments that are built too close to freeways or are built on land that sits lower than most of the surrounding structures and roads.

✣ Home buyers can carefully consider whether they want to live in a home that is precariously built on a hillside with no rear support but has a view to die for.

✣ Understand the difference between architectural whimsy versus design that seeks to optimize balance and fluidity.

✣ Bathrooms should always be designed with a low profile in terms of location and visibility.

✣ Homes builders can minimize the square footage of the bedroom space built over the garage. In other words, if a bedroom is only partially located over the garage it will minimize the disturbance to the bedroom and in particular the sleeping area from the instability of opening and closing the garage door, parking cars and the addition of exhaust fumes.

✣ Location and housing for utilities, security systems, entertainment systems including satellite dishes and all the technical conveniences (smart houses) should be well planned so as not to locate them near sleeping areas, in particular, the wall where the head of the bed is located.

These are just a few suggestions that can make a big impact on the strength and integrity of a home and its feng shui. In 2004 California Assembly Member Yee introduced a measure urging the "California Building Standards Commission to adopt building standards that promote Feng Shui Principles and publish these standards in the California Building Standards Code." You can read the text from Bill ACR 144 in the appendix of this book. The formal language used to describe and explain feng shui is interesting however, like most things in life, education and personal responsibility for feng shui design will be more effective than legislation.

Concluding Remarks

Feng shui begins with the basic and fundamental approach of clearing clutter and creating a harmonious and balanced arrangement in the living space. It then graduates to the assessment or selection of a property based on the shape of the lot and layout of the home, including the surroundings and movement of energy. This more sophisticated application of feng shui can also include compass orientation, water placement and cycles of time. Lastly, but certainly not least, the layer of intentional and symbolic décor is added to further enhance the living space.

It is always important to keep in mind that the *cumulative* effect of weak features in a house is what ultimately undermines strong feng shui. Minor undesirable features will not have an influence on the overall energy of the home. Most feng shui weaknesses can be counterbalanced by understanding and applying the guidelines from this book. I have come to appreciate that beauty and aesthetics have the greatest influence over some of the most challenging feng shui floor plans. Even the effects of the worst floor plan can be minimized with an intentional and deliberate design concept. Through creativity and the observance of beauty and aesthetics an environment can instantly be transformed and its deficiencies transcended.

"Fate can be shaped if its laws are known"

—Tao Te Ching

The essence of feng shui is the observation and adherence to the laws and principles that govern nature. Firstly, there is the recognition that, whether visible or invisible, gross or subtle energy expresses itself in the environment in a myriad of ways. Our interaction with our environments is both a formative and influential process that works both ways. We infuse our environments with our thoughts and our environments continually activate and elicit responses from us. The understanding that the organic interaction with your living space can be intentionally planned and directed to benefit your life is a powerful connection to make.

Portions of a quote from Charles F. Haanel, when describing the correct use of the mind, reminded me of how I describe the benefits associated with the practice of feng shui. It is like casting a large net in order to better capture life's opportunities.

"He sees opportunities for success to which he was heretofore blind. He recognizes possibilities which before had no meaning for him. He attracts to himself new and successful associates, and this in turn changes his environment; so that by this simple exercise of thought, a man changes not only himself, but his environment, circumstances and conditions."

An acquaintance of mine once remarked that she credited her understanding and practice of feng shui for the remarkable timing of the events in her life. Events and opportunities always seemed to be so well timed for her.

Many years ago, I did a consultation for an elderly woman. We worked on many aspects of her small dwelling to make it and herself stronger. I had no idea about her financial circumstances at the time but she called me the next day and told me that she was being crushed by medical bills and that after our consultation she received notice that the insurance company was finally going to pay all the outstanding bills. That day I concluded that when you unblock the energy in an environment, create space and flow, and to the best of your ability, unburden yourself, the outcome can only be one of liberation. Here is to your freedom, health and quality of life. May you thrive in your homes and prosper.

MaryAnn Russell

火 水 木 土 金

Appendix A

Yin Yang

Yin Yang Theory - how it applies in everyday life

Yin and yang simply expresses the dualistic or contrasting nature of **all** that we experience in life. For every one thing there is its corresponding opposite. *The balancing of the opposites is one way to define what feng shui seeks to accomplish in our living spaces.* If there is excessive yang energy in the bedroom due to décor or architectural design the occupants may suffer from poor sleep or other difficulties. Recognizing that the bedroom should have more yin, still and restful qualities rather than active yang energy, one would seek to correct the imbalance in the bedroom.

In every beginning feng shui class or book you will see lists of yin qualities and yang qualities:

Yin	Yang
Darkness	Brightness
Things female	Things male
Moon	Sun
Still	Active
Night	Day
Earth	Heaven
Cold	Hot
Autumn & Winter	Spring & Summer
Small & weak	Large & strong
Solid	Active
Receptive	Expressive
Inward & Interior	Outward & Exterior
Front of the body	Back of the body
Contraction	Expansion
Holding and containing energy	Expressing and releasing energy

The Feng Shui Factor

Rather than seeing yin and yang separately it is more accurate to see yin and yang as phases or cycles. In the seasons, winter, (great yin) with the qualities of stillness and hibernation it is the time where all of nature moves *inward*. At the first sign of spring the strength of yin is lessened and the movement begins. The yang energy starts to activate and stimulate growth and life. Summer is most characterized by yang energy; during this phase we have the peak of activity, all of nature is sizzling. When autumn arrives there is a decline in energy and after the harvest all of nature starts to pull inward as it moves toward the completion of the yearly cycle.

The most practical application of yin and yang is through observation. One can observe the energy of a particular day, some days are more yang and support high productivity, meeting and networking with people. All the activities are external (yang). Other days are more yin, when ideas are germinating, time is taken to nurture oneself, spend quiet time indoors with the family. Having a full day of appointments and activities on a cold winter day when the energy is very yin is quite a different experience then on a bright and sunny June day when the energy in nature is high, active and external (yang). Understanding the cycles and qualities of yin and yang can help us to understand the phenomenal flux of our life experience, as it relates to people and events. One thing we all can observe is people in business and the media. It's not unusual to see someone at the so-called top of his or her career or stardom come crashing down. A person can be involved in so many projects, allowing a yang phase of expansion to continue without balance so that the eventual contraction (yin) will result. The contraction can express itself in seemingly harsh ways such as bankruptcy, health crisis, a failed relationship or a destroyed reputation. This is why the balance of yin and yang is so important because nature will correct itself if we don't.

I found it a very interesting decision by Martha Stewart

whether justly or unjustly to fulfill her prison sentence in the winter yin cycle. Martha Stewart is all things holiday and festive. Why would she make the decision to serve her time during the holidays? I realized that according to the natural cycle, the winter is when things naturally hibernate and die. Was her plan intentional to emerge in the spring when seeds are planted for new beginnings? I thought this was a very astute plan to use the natural cycles of nature for support. When I mentioned this to a friend she remarked that this is how gardeners think and plan. By observing the expression of yin and yang in everyday life you can sharpen your perception of your environment, people and events.

You cannot discuss feng shui without a well-grounded understanding of yin and yang. Terminology that describes the environment as activate and energized (yang) or still and quiet (yin). Let us now look at some obvious indicators of where either yin or yang may be out of balance in a home. Remember, there are many ways in which these imbalances can be corrected or counterbalanced.

Some of the most common visible things that can contribute to extreme yin energy in a home are:

1. Trees, shrubs and vines encroaching on the house and blocking the natural sunlight.

2. Dead plants.

3. A dark entry way and poorly lit rooms.

4. A basement or subterranean room.

5. Using too many dark colors in the décor.

6. A house in disrepair.

7. Artwork and symbols in the home that are not life affirming.

8. Any exterior structure that may be overpowering the house.

9. Prolonged Illness and death.

10. Living next to a hospital, mortuary or graveyard.

Some of the most common visible things that can contribute to extreme yang energy in a home are:

1. Too many windows and doors.

2. Floor to ceiling glass walls.

3. 180 degree view.

4. An overly open floor plan.

5. A high rise or a home built on a mountain top that is overly exposed to the elements.

6. An overly exposed ocean front home .

7. Bright busy wall color and décor, especially reds & bright whites.

8. Homes situated on corner lots without the proper landscaping to absorb the street traffic on two sides of the house.

9. Close proximity to a busy street, business, airport, fire department, school (in these cases the energy of the home is also disturbed).

It is important to remember nothing is entirely yin or entirely yang; all things are comprised of both energies. For example, even in light of the descriptions above a home in the Pacific Northwest, part of the US where it is cloudy and raining many months out of the year, will need to adjust their feng shui placement for the climate. Using reds, bright colors and enlivening light fixtures will balance the home during the cloudy rainy months. The occupants will be less susceptible to low moods and depression. In contrast, the same décor would be much too yang for a home in the desert. In a desert climate using earth tones and cool, calm colors and well-placed water features will balance the fire of the desert.

Appendix B

Electromagnetic Fields

When high electromagnetic fields are present in an environment there is an ambient feeling of compression, constriction and agitation which, over time, may express itself in a host of symptoms for the occupants. Restlessness, cloudy thinking, headaches, fatigue and irritability are just a few examples. The technological advances of our time are remarkable but we have to consider the impact on our health and well-being. The modern feng shui consultation must include some education about the potential health risks that are a by-product of our modern times. A feng shui consultant should be equipped with a Tri-Field meter to detect high electromagnetic fields in the sleeping areas of the bedroom, in particular the wall where the headboard of the bed is positioned.

If high readings are detected follow these steps to help determine the source:

1. Unplug electrical appliances in close proximity to the head of the bed. Radios, alarm clocks, night stand lamps and electric blankets are often the source of the high reading.

Note: A safe distance for appliances is an arm's length from your head. Electric blankets are not recommended.

2. If the readings are still high the electricity to the home should be shut off at the circuit breaker and another meter reading should be taken. This will determine if the electromagnetic field comes from the home itself or from the public utility equipment.

3. If the meter does not detect a field the source is within the wiring or cabling of the house.

4. If the meter still has a high reading then the source is likely the power company's equipment.

An electrician or other qualified professional can help you find solutions for your wiring.

If you suspect that power lines above or below ground may be "dirty" the power company should come out, at no charge to you. They will test the lines and equipment to see if all the returns are clean. The utility companies are responsible for their equipment. Having said that, the power company's criteria for what they consider unsafe electromagnetic fields may be somewhat liberal.

I find it interesting that the Southern California Edison Company occasionally inserts an EMF (electro magnetic fields) brochure into their monthly bill entitled, "Understanding EMF". It has some helpful tips even though it reads like a disclaimer.

Following are excerpts from the Edison brochure:

Can EMF Harm Your Health?

Electric and magnetic fields are present wherever electricity flows around appliances and power lines, and in offices, schools and homes. Many researchers believe that if there is a risk of adverse health effects from usual residential exposures to EMF, it is probably just at the detection limit of human health studies; nonetheless, the possible risk warrants further investigation. The varying results from epidemiological studies linking estimated EMF exposures with childhood leukemia are consistent with a weak effect. **Laboratory experiments have shown that EMF can cause changes in living cells.** There is little evidence that these changes suggest any risk to human health.

The results from many research studies have been reported by both national and California EMF research programs to find out if EMF poses any health risk. Given the uncertainty of the issue, the medical and scientific communities have been unable to determine that usual residential exposures to EMF cause health effects or to establish any standard or level of exposure that is known to be either safe or harmful.

What You Can Do

The CPUC's 1993 decision (0.93-11-013) addressed possible EMF health effects from electric utility facilities. In a situation of scientific uncertainty and public concern, the CPUC felt it appropriate for utilities to take no-cost and low-cost measures where feasible to reduce EMF exposure from new or upgraded Utility facilities. You, too, may want to take no-cost and low-cost measures to reduce your EMF exposure at home and at work.

Human studies have not produced a consensus about any health benefits from changing the way people use electric appliances. But, if you feel reducing your EMF exposure would be beneficial, you can increase your distance from electric appliances and or limit the amount of time you use appliances at home or at work.

For instance, you can place phone answering machines and electric clocks away from the head of your bed. Increasing your distance from these and other appliances such as televisions, computer monitors and microwave ovens can reduce your EMF exposure.

You can also reduce your EMF exposure by limiting the time you spend using personal appliances such as hair dryers, electric razors, heating pads and electric blankets. You may also want to limit the time you spend using electric cooking appliances.

You can locate the sources of EMF in your work environment, and spend break time in lower-field areas.

It is not known whether such actions will have any impact on your health.

Appendix C

Life Aspirations

The "life aspiration" aspect of feng shui tends to pique the interest of people, while at the same time, causing the most controversy about where these locations are in the home. Some feng shui schools don't emphasize the life aspirations; other schools have an alternate arrangement of the bagua and then orient it in relationship to the front door. Other schools relate the life aspirations to the compass directions. When a section of the house is missing, it is viewed as a challenge to the corresponding life aspiration. In the examples below compare the grid of life aspirations to the house shapes to determine which life aspiration is missing or weakened.

Each of the Life Aspirations can be enhanced by its associated element placed in its respective location (see Chapter Five for suggestions) as well as the placement of something symbolic. The following is a description of each aspiration as well as some symbolic suggestions for creating a deeper connection and focus on a particular life area. The symbolic remedies are used to connect and sharpen your focus and intention on each of the life aspirations.

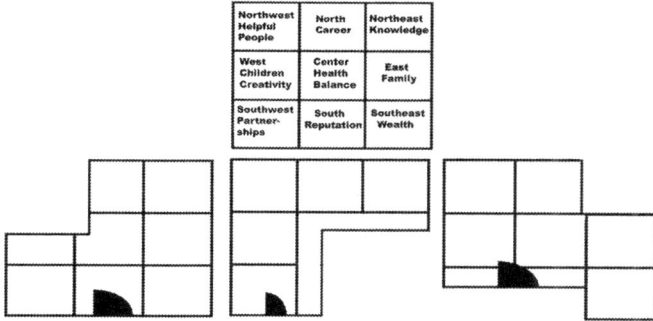

Northwest Helpful People	North Career	Northeast Knowledge
West Children Creativity	Center Health Balance	East Family
Southwest Partnerships	South Reputation	Southeast Wealth

Career - North - 1 Water

Your career is supported in the north—the colors are blue and black. Objects of art that symbolize water are wavey, curved and depict movement. Any type of continual motion represents the water element. The tortoise symbolizes the north; you can place a metal tortoise in the north to support your career and place a crystal globe on your desk to expand your connections. Your office will be enhanced by putting your accreditations, degrees, business cards and vision for your career on the north wall. In this area of the home make sure that nothing is in disrepair or cluttered symbolizing a broken down or stagnant career.

Partnerships - Southwest - 2 Earth

The southwest is the direction that supports relationships. It is characterized by unions and partnerships. Focusing on this area fosters the connection between the **two**. Wedding as well as current photographs of you and your partner are best placed in the southwest. Any object of art that represents unions will enhance this area, while lone, contemplative figures will not be suitable. Pay close attention to using **pairs** of things rather than odd numbers in this area.

Family - East - 3 Wood

The east's influence is on the unity and health of the family. The color green represents growth and expansion as does cylindrical shapes and pillars like the red woods or island palms. Always make sure the plants and trees in and around your property are healthy but not overgrown, or obstructing doors or windows. Placing family photographs in the east will foster unity and family cohesion. Symbols of longevity and artwork that depict strength and vitality are all suitable for the east. If you are working on a health goal, placing something meaningful that represents the accomplishment of that goal is key.

Wealth - Southeast - 4 Wood

It has been said, "That a person can do more good with money than without it." Prosperity and abundance are connected with the southeast. A **tree** made of the golden citrine gem is a timely piece to place in this area. Sparkling money pots, colorful piggy banks and anything that enhances your personal connection to prosperity.

Health & Balance - Center - 5 Earth

The center is the area of balance and health. All of the eight directions connect to the center, the earth element for the center is depicted as a landscape of rolling hills. Avoid putting water in this area. The Tai chi symbol and balanced scales are extremely powerful symbols for the center. When the **center area** of the home has too much activity, place something that has a calm solid quality or that symbolizes stability.

Networking - Helpful People - Northwest - 6 Metal

The northwest influences helpful people and travel. All successful people in life have a network of supportive people. This direction supports the kind and quality of help you get from people. This includes all professional people and the services you use, including teachers, mentors and benefactors. Symbolically represent your network of people and travel plans with photos, business cards, books, travel brochures, maps, globes, art and artifacts from memorable trips.

Children and Creativity - West - 7 Metal

The colors of the west are white, silver and metallic gold. The shape of metal is round, oval and arched. Creativity, your children's general well being, activities and academics are influenced by the west. To increase the focus on creative pursuits use the west area of the home or west direction (micro direction) of your office or studio to represent your high priority projects. If you have children, age appropriate art depicting children, or their own artwork, will help nurture their creativity.

Knowledge - Northeast - 8 Earth

The earth colors are yellow, beige, brown and tan. The earth shape is square. The northeast is a very powerful area for personal development and academics. By enhancing this area you will be supporting your receptivity to learning and increase your intellectual capacity for all academic pursuits. In a home, this will be the ideal location for a study or library. The northeast is the mountain that is strong, still and quiet. Bookshelves can be put along the northeast wall, anything that you are currently studying or knowledge that you intend to pursue. Avoid placing water in this area, it is the place of the mountain. Gold objects of art and accents in gold are recommend for the northeast.

Reputation & Fame - South - 9 Fire

The success of a person or business depends on their good name and reputation. Name recognition, how well you are known and what people associate with your name or company, is vital. All shades of red and triangular shapes belong to the south. The phoenix is the bird of the south and galloping horses energize a swift rise to high profile positions. Symbolic enhancements include: awards, trophies, commendations and anything related with you being recognized for your work and accomplishments. In general, that with which you want to be known and associated will be most suited to the south. An individual must be clear about how much recognition is desired and what kind.

Note: Do not use symbolic enhancements in the bathroom.

APPENDIX D

Compass Reading

To determine the basic orientation of your property follow these steps:

1. Acquire a compass from a sporting goods store or other outdoor outfitter. A medium priced needle or digital compass will be adequate. Do not use a GPS (global positioning system), because you are measuring "magnetic" orientation not satellite.

2. Remove all metal jewelry (rings, watches and bracelets).

3. For purposes of determining the basic orientation of your home, position yourself in the front of the house with your back to the front door.

4. Hold the compass waist high and level to obtain your first reading (make a note of it)

5. Take two more readings from different positions along the same "line" of the house, i.e. with your back to the house. By taking three readings you can feel confident that your compass reading is consistent within 15 degrees. If you have inconsistent readings there may be some electrical interference or you may

be standing in the vicinity of metal pipes. Move locations and determine your general compass orientation.

6. Draw a grid and place it over your floor plan to determine the compass location of each area of your home.

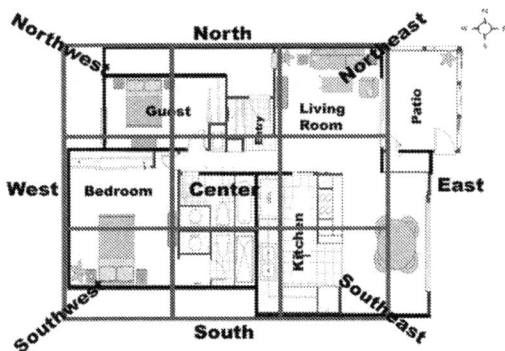

The Feng Shui Factor

APPENDIX E

Bagua Mirrors

The word bagua is actually two words ba (pronounced "baw") and gua (pronounced "gwa"). Ba is the number eight and gua means section, bagua literally means eight sections. Each of the sections denotes the eight compass directions along with other symbolic representation related to the earthly plane. The bagua mirror should only be used on the exterior of a home or building and never in the interior. In feng shui this is considered a very strong image and should be placed with care. If the mirror in the center is convex it can be used to distance an undesirable structure (poison arrow) or unwanted energy. If the mirror is concave, it can be used to invert an overpowering or other undesirable structure.

Appendix F

Assembly Concurrent Resolution No. 144--
Relative to Feng Shui

LEGISLATIVE COUNSEL'S DIGEST

BILL NUMBER: ACR 144

INTRODUCED BILL TEXT INTRODUCED BY:
Assembly Member Yee JANUARY 5, 2004

This measure would urge the California Building Standards Commission to adopt building standards that promote Feng Shui principles and publish these standards in the California Building Standards Code.

WHEREAS, Feng Shui is a natural earth science that reveals how people are affected by their immediate surroundings, and its core philosophy states humankind must live in harmony with the environment; and WHEREAS, The practice of Feng Shui originated 4,000 years ago in ancient China when palaces and senior official residences were built according to Feng Shui principles that ensured that the royal families and senior court officials enjoyed harmony and high vitality living in a positive energy environment; and WHEREAS, Feng Shui means wind (Feng) and water (Shui), and Chinese practitioners have focused their studies on obtaining the most benefit from the understanding of the flow of energies in the earth known as chi; and WHEREAS, Feng Shui advocates living in harmony with the Earth's environment and its energy lines, so that there is a proper balance between the forces of nature; and WHEREAS, Feng Shui is widely practiced in China, Taiwan, Singapore, and Malaysia, and it is regarded as a vital part of everyday life in many parts of Asia; and WHEREAS, Several western companies practice Feng Shui, including Citibank, N. M. Rothschild, Shell, and Sime Darby, and the principles of Feng Shui have become increasingly popular in western culture with fashion designers such as Donna Karan and Tommy Hilfiger integrating it in their showrooms, and entrepreneur Donald Trump consulting Feng Shui experts at his properties; and WHEREAS, The structure of a building can affect a person's mood, which can influence a person's behavior, which, in turn, can determine the success of a person's personal and professional relationships, and the aim of Feng Shui architecture is to study how the environment in which people live may affect their lives, and influence their quality of life; now, therefore, be it resolved by the Assembly of the State of California, the Senate thereof concurring, That the Legislature of the State of California urges the California Building Standards Commission to adopt building standards that promote Feng Shui principles and publish these building standards in the California Building Standards Code; and be it further Resolved, That the Chief Clerk of the Assembly transmit copies of this resolution to the author for appropriate distribution.

ACKNOWLEDGEMENTS

I have to express my deepest appreciation, gratitude and love for my husband Richard who is my support and touchstone. My deepest gratitude for my brilliant and beautiful daughter Amy, for me it is a privilege to be her mother. They are both the greatest gifts and blessings in my life.

I want to thank my mother Aida Marrone for her love, support and encouragement. She is truly an example of grace, beauty and dignity. I want to thank my sister Gala for her encouragement and example of courage and creativity.

My appreciation is extended to all my family and friends, in particular Elaine Hogue and Sheila Wright for their encouragement and confidence in me. I want to thank my childhood friend Karen Le Masters for her support and thoughtful viewpoints.

For all the pioneers and professionals who have aspired to explore human potential to its fullest, I want to thank you. I want to thank Bill Harris' for his research on brain wave technology (Holosync) and all the work of "The Centerpointe Research Institute". Mr. Harris is an outstanding model of excellence in business. I would also like to thank "Family

Systems Research Group" for their ongoing research, development and work to improve the human condition.

Finally, I want to express my appreciation to my clients who have allowed me into their homes and businesses. I have learned so much from you and been enriched by your lives.

ABOUT THE AUTHOR

MaryAnn Russell is an expert in the field of environmental energy. She has studied all the major schools of feng shui. For over a decade the focus of her research and practice has been on the feng shui factors that truly influence the quality of people's lives.

She distills the theories and concepts of feng shui and translates them into practical and useful knowledge for her clients. For years she has worked with home owners, business owners, realtors, investors, designers and builders to maximize the potential of their environments.

MaryAnn is dedicated to exploring the limitless aspects of personal development and human potential.

She resides in Southern California with her family where she focuses on her passion for homes, remodeling and property renovation.

"The focus of my practice is to make feng shui relevant, practical and useful so that people can gain the greatest possible benefit from their living spaces."

For more information contact:

MaryAnn Russell

714.842.7728

www.fengshuifactor.com

INDEX

www.ingramcontent.com/pod-product-compliance
Lightning Source LLC
Chambersburg PA
CBHW052006090426
42741CB00008B/1577